Anti-libertarianism

Advocates of the free market claim that it is the only economic mechanism capable of respecting and furthering human freedom. Socialism, they say, has been thoroughly discredited. Most libertarians treat the state in anything other than its minimal, 'nightwatchman' form as a repressive embodiment of evil. Some reject the state altogether.

But is the 'free market idea' a rationally defensible belief? Or have its proponents failed to examine the philosophical roots of their so-called freedom? *Anti-libertarianism* reconsiders the theoretical libertarian stance, starting with an analysis of the model of 'mutually beneficial' exchanges which is at the core of libertarian thinking. Alan Haworth's book is a sceptical exploration of the concepts and arguments which form the tenets of free market politics. He offers the view that libertarianism is little more than an unfounded, quasi-religious statement of faith: a market romance. Moreover, libertarianism is exposed as profoundly antithetical to the very freedom which it purports to advance.

This controversial book is for anyone interested in the cultural and political impact of free market policies on the modern world. It will be useful to students and specialists of political and economic theory, social science and philosophy.

Alan Haworth is Senior Lecturer in Philosophy at the University of North London.

Anti-libertarianism

Markets, philosophy and myth

Alan Haworth

London and New York

First published 1994
by Routledge
11 New Fetter Lane, London EC4P 4EE

Simultaneously published in the USA and Canada
by Routledge
29 West 35th Street, New York, NY 10001

Typeset in Baskerville by the EPPP Group at Routledge
Printed and bound in Great Britain by
Mackays of Chatham PLC, Chatham, Kent

British Library Cataloguing in Publication Data
A catalogue record for this book is available from the British Library
ISBN 0–415–08253–6 (hb) ISBN 0–415–08254–4 (pb)

Library of Congress Cataloging in Publication Data
Haworth, Alan, 1944-
Anti-libertarianism : markets, philosophy and myth / Alan Haworth.
p. cm.
Includes bibliographical references and index.

ISBN 0–415–08253–6 (hb). – ISBN 0–415–08254–4 (pb)
1. Libertarianism. I. Title.
HB95.H385 1994   93–37964
330. 12´6–dc20   CIP

For my father; for Rowan; for Matthew

Contents

Preface and acknowledgements

I wrote this with my friends more than anyone else in mind. Like most intelligent people, they have been variously bewildered, puzzled, intrigued, discouraged, disaffected, changed around and moved about thanks to the dominance in our public life of the notion that there is something noble about something or other usually referred to as the 'free market'. I hope they like the book, and that they will share my belief that, if you're going to cut some sinister thing down to size, the first thing you have to do is analyse and anatomise.

Otherwise, there isn't a great deal to say by way of preface that wouldn't just repeat what I say in the opening chapter; so let me just warmly thank all the individuals who have been so supportive over the last year while I have been writing. Unfortunately, there isn't space to mention everyone by name, but the following definitely deserve mention here.

There are – first – my professional colleagues at the University of North London. I owe a special debt of gratitude to the members of the Research and Staff Development Committee (Faculty of Humanities and Teacher Education) who decided to award me the relief from teaching without which it would have been impossible to complete the book on time. Let me add – because I know that it is conventional and expected for the recipients of such awards to acknowledge them in the way I just have – that I mean that more than formally. I am deeply appreciative, and I realise how difficult it is for such committees to reach decisions in these straitened times. I am similarly appreciative of the way my colleagues, mainly my fellow philosophy teachers but also many others within the faculty, have supported me informally. I know that everyone has gone to great lengths to make sure that I have had the time to write. And, while I'm on the subject, I would like to thank the students, present and past, with whom I've had the pleasure of sharing my classes on political philosophy. I wonder who has learnt most from whom, and I count myself very lucky to have spent the greater part of my working life in such an interesting environment.

Second, there are friends and family to thank. If I were to try to mention everyone, I might miss someone out. Therefore, I shall mention no one by name except, that is, for Rowan, to whom I am especially grateful for her having assumed the role of live-in domestic engineer and child psychologist on a one-to-one basis over the last few weeks of writing. I guess that this sort of thing doesn't come too easily to a committed feminist.

Third, I am indebted to David Lloyd-Thomas and Andrew Wright, each of whom took the trouble to go through an earlier draft and make comments, despite the fact that they are both extremely busy people. It is impossible to express just how helpful I found this. I am sure that the book is much better than it would have been had it not been for the careful attention they paid it. I should add – as is usual – that the responsibility for remaining mistakes and infelicities remains entirely my own. Finally, I should like to thank Leigh Wilson of Routledge for her helpful comments and suggestions.

Alan Haworth
University of North London

A NOTE ON REFERENCING

I have used the Harvard system, even where I refer to passages in Locke's *Second Treatise* and Wittgenstein's *Philosophical Investigations*. In these cases it is customary to reference differently, by directing the reader to paragraphs noted in a certain way in the original manuscripts. However, I have thought it better to employ a standard practice throughout.

Part I

The struggle of man against power is the struggle of memory against forgetting.

Milan Kundera, *The Book of Laughter and Forgetting*

The work of the philosopher consists in assembling reminders for a particular purpose.

Ludwig Wittgenstein, *Philosophical Investigations*

Chapter 1

Libertarianism - anti-libertarianism

'Libertarianism' is a word with two meanings. In the earlier of the two it refers, exactly as one might expect, to any body of attitudes or ideas in which central importance is attached to freedom. In that sense of 'libertarian', the arguments of this book are libertarian. More recently, however, the word has come to refer to something altogether different and more specific, namely a certain assertively right-wing, pro-free market philosophy. This book's subject is libertarianism in the second sense. Its aim is to outline that doctrine's main arguments and to expose its shaky structure to public view. This book is thus – and in the latter sense of 'libertarian' – anti-libertarian.

Libertarians (of the second sort) maintain three central theses. First, as indicated, they maintain that the market (or 'free' market) is good. Indeed, libertarians of this sort make *enormous* claims on behalf of the free market, the very least of these – and the most apparently pragmatic – being that the market is the distributive mechanism which ensures the satisfaction of needs and preferences most effectively. For most libertarians of this type, though, the market is more than that – much more. It is the nearest thing there is to the realisation of the perfect moral order on Earth. (I do not exaggerate.) Second, libertarians (of the sort who form the subject of this book) hold that the state – except in its minimal or 'nightwatchman' form, if that – is evil. Third, as its chosen *nom de guerre* suggests, libertarian doctrine asserts that freedom is of supreme importance. It is this third thesis which acts as the crossbar, or strut, connecting the first with the second. Thus, the market is held to be good principally because, or so it is claimed, only the free market can supply the fertile soil in which the fragile flower of freedom can bloom. The state's intrinsically evil character is correspondingly held to flow from the fact that any (other than minimal) state is necessarily freedom's iron enemy.

The foregoing theses will be extremely familiar to most readers, including readers who weren't previously aware that – within philosophy if not elsewhere – these ideas tend to be labelled 'libertarian'. This very familiarity ought to be sufficient in itself to demonstrate the extent to which libertarian ideas have recently come to supply the small coin for a certain debased ideological currency. I would put it even more strongly. Libertarianism may not be the most subtle philosophical doctrine extant, but, with socialism temporarily out of fashion, it is – at least arguably – the political philosophy which has brought the most influence to bear on practical affairs over recent years. I should like to think that this gives the arguments I present here some point.

Introductory chapters should be short, and only four more remarks are necessary here. First, I treat libertarianism thematically; that is, I have tried to give it the best run for its money I can through an analysis of the best arguments I know for its three central theses. This means that I have, of necessity, concentrated on certain writers rather than others. I haven't even tried to give a full synoptic account of the available literature.[1] I am sure that, as a consequence, some self-styled libertarians – for example, the acolytes of the various think-tanks, alliances, institutes and foundations so fashionable these days – will object that I have missed the point, that some of the writers I discuss are insufficiently libertarian to be counted amongst the truly elect. But objections along these lines would themselves be beside the point because the purpose of political philosophy is to explore the logical and argumentative structures which underlie the positions people take up, not to categorise or itemise who takes them.

Second, it is possible that some readers will be surprised to learn that the underlying arguments exist; that is, that libertarianism has a 'serious' side at all. Libertarian catch-phrases have become so much the stock in trade of a certain style of propaganda that readers may be forgiven for having gained the impression that libertarianism is just that branch of the rag-trade which caters for those members of the pin-striped classes who wish to appear intellectually respectably dressed. (Familiar sloganised false dichotomies, 'the state should not provide, but enable' or 'privatisation not coercion is the answer', are examples of such catchphrases.)[2] But it does have a serious side. Libertarianism has some powerful exponents and can claim, with at least some justification, a distinguished ancestry in the work of John Locke and Adam Smith among others. I concentrate on this, although it would have been interesting – very interesting – to explore the way libertarian theory is processed by the propaganda machine. Sadly, one can only do so much in a given space, but, by way of compensation, I have made do by awarding Sir Keith Joseph a small walk-on part in the earlier sections of this narrative.[3]

Third, just in case anyone is in danger of getting the wrong impression, let me itemise some claims I am *not* about to make. For a start, (1) I am not an envious sort of person, nor am I greatly enamoured of envy as a motive. Therefore, I am not about to base an argument on that motive. (2) Unlike Procrustes (who seems to be a favourite bogeyman of the Right),[4] I do not get my kicks from the amputation of other people's limbs or from stretching my victims on racks, nor do I recommend such activities as exemplary. (If I do have a Greek hero it is not Procrustes, but Ulysses, who liberated his comrades by blinding the giant cyclops which was holding them captive.)[5] (3) I am not a political aesthete, and I do not look forward to the realisation of some totalitarian nightmare on earth, a world in which a well-ordered 'collectivist' machine authoritatively orders every human movement. (4) I do not believe that freedom is equivalent to rational self-mastery, nor that true freedom is a question of acting in accordance with the desires or dictates of some rational, 'higher' self. (5) I do not believe that all values are logically compatible or that in some harmonious order they can (will) all be perfectly realised. In fact, I am strongly persuaded of the reverse. In short, I am not open to the accusations routinely levelled by the philosophical Right at their critics; so routinely that many readers will have already assumed that I am about to make the very claims I have just denied.

Such readers should take warning and – my fourth point – they should take particular warning that I am absolutely *not* against freedom. On the contrary, I am for it. Libertarians (in the second sense of the word) think they are for freedom but they don't know what freedom is. In reality, their doctrine is so contrary to freedom that it ought to be entitled 'anti-libertarianism'. The thief comes in innocent disguise, but the beautiful garment is stolen. (The Right are good at that sort of thing.) So, if you want to make your copy of this book read more accurately, you should delete 'libertarian' and 'libertarianism' throughout, substituting 'anti-libertarian' and 'anti-libertarianism' as you go. For 'anti-libertarianism', etc., you should substitute 'anti-anti-libertarianism'. Unfortunately, this would make the book cumbersome to read, so I haven't followed the advice myself except in my choice of title, where my subject is named according to its true nature.

Chapter 2

Market romances I
Nuts and bolts

As for the general conclusion to which the arguments I present here tend, it's a fairly safe bet that Adam Smith's two most quoted remarks are these:

> He [every individual] generally, indeed, neither intends to promote the publick interest, nor knows how much he is promoting it. By preferring the support of domestic to that of foreign industry, he intends only his own security; and by directing that industry in such a manner as its produce may be of the greatest value, he intends only his own gain, and he is in this, as in many other cases, led by an invisible hand to promote an end which was no part of his intention. Nor is it always the worse for the society that it was no part of it. By pursuing his own interest he frequently promotes that of the society more effectually than when he really intends to promote it.
>
> (1976: 477–8)

and;

> All systems either of preference or restraint, therefore, being thus completely taken away, the obvious and simple system of natural liberty establishes itself of its own accord.
>
> (1976: 208)

If it is a characteristic of religion to invoke awe at the magical properties with which some supposed immanent order is allegedly imbued, then these statements – with their exhortation to seek grace through surrender to the hand of a higher law – qualify as religious. All will be well, and all will be well – if only. It turns out on analysis that much libertarian theory is little more than this; an unfounded quasi-religious statement of faith. It is, as I should like to put it, a *market romance*. (More sceptical readers will have suspected as much all along, of course.)

However – and naturally enough – libertarianism claims to be more. It claims to be a body of truth founded upon an appeal to reason and firm evidence. Specifically, many libertarians hold (1) that the market exchange is a *paradigmatic exemplar* of freedom, as it is of want-satisfaction also. They hold (2) that a pure free market (or 'capitalist') economy is 'simply', or 'nothing more than' the sum or aggregate of all the market exchanges which actually take place between individuals within a given set. (I shall call this 'the reducibility thesis'.) For such libertarians both *the freedom thesis* and *the invisible hand thesis* (so named after Smith's remark quoted above) are closely logically related to, if not directly entailed by (1) and (2) taken together.

To begin at the beginning we should consider this relationship. Of course, I am not saying that all libertarians hold exactly the same view – and in the later sections of this book I shall discuss more sophisticated variants – but there is, nevertheless, a core position, a sort of 'standard' version of the doctrine. We should take this first and consider the discrete components, the nuts and bolts which – according to libertarians – hold the market structure together. These are bilateral market exchanges between individuals.

1 THE MARKET EXCHANGE

So, what is a market exchange? Well, suppose that I have more of some thing, A, than I want and that you, likewise, have more of some other thing, B, than you want. You would like some of my A, and I would like some of your B. It should be obvious that the solution to our problem is to swap or exchange; my spare A for your extra B. So, we swap.

The notion seems simple and unmysterious enough, but for some it comes laden with high moral import. For libertarians the two most salient features of this type of case are, first, that the exchange is *free*; second, that it is *mutually beneficial*. To take the former point, it should be clear enough that – other things being equal – the exchange will not take place unless we both agree to participate, and that it therefore involves consent; that, since we 'could have chosen' not to participate, the exchange is 'voluntary'; that we participate 'of our own free will'; that no one 'coerces' us into exchanging. The exchange is a 'free exchange' in these respects at least. To take the latter point, the exchange is mutually beneficial in the sense that, after it has taken place, each of us now has something he or she previously wanted but lacked. We are both, in a phrase, 'better off' than we were immediately before.

The literature of libertarianism is packed with such stories, each de-signed to illustrate the above points. Let me give a few well-known examples, beginning with Milton Friedman's invitation – early on in *Capitalism and Freedom* – to consider:

a number of independent households – a collection of Robinson Crusoes, as it were. Each household uses the resources it controls to produce goods and services that it exchanges for goods and services produced by other households, on terms mutually acceptable to the two parties to the bargain. . . . Since the household always has the alternative of producing directly for itself, it need not enter into any exchange unless it benefits from it. Hence, no exchange will take place unless both parties do benefit from it.

(1962: 13)

Friedman draws from this the moral that, 'co-operation is thereby achieved without coercion'. Consider, too, Murray Rothbard on the subject of buying a newspaper for a dime:

I transfer my ownership of the dime to the news dealer and he transfers ownership of the paper to me. We do this because, under the division of labor, I calculate that the paper is worth more to me than the dime, while the news dealer prefers the dime to keeping the paper.

(1973: 41–2)

Rothbard describes this as a 'mutually beneficial two-person exchange', as he would no doubt also describe the exchanges between Wilt Chamberlain, the famous basketball player, and each of his fans in Robert Nozick's example. In Nozick's story, Chamberlain signs a contract which states that, for each home game, 'twenty-five cents from the price of each ticket of admission goes to him'.

The season starts, and people cheerfully attend his team's games; they buy their tickets, each time dropping a separate twenty-five cents of their admission price into a special box with Chamberlain's name on it. They are excited about seeing him play; it is worth the total admission price to them . . . in one season, one million persons attend his home games, and Wilt Chamberlain winds up with $250,000.

(Nozick 1974: 161)

So, the exchanges are mutually beneficial – Chamberlain gets a fortune and the fans are entertained – and also, as Nozick stresses, 'Each of these persons *chose* to give twenty-five cents of their money to Chamberlain'. All this echoes another of Adam Smith's well-known remarks, that 'It is not from the benevolence of the butcher, the brewer, or the baker that we expect our dinner, but from their regard to their own interest', which occurs in the context of a discussion of bargaining. As Smith says:

> Give me that which I want, and you shall have this which you want, is the meaning of every such offer, and it is in this manner that we obtain from one another the far greater part of those good offices which we stand in need of.
>
> (1976: 18)

2 COMPLICATIONS

It is noticeable that problems arise even here, even though this narrative has hardly begun; for things in this simple world of brewers, bakers, newsvendors and basketball jocks, with its folksy, *Saturday Evening Post* aura, are less innocent than they initially appear. Let us pause to note a few complications.

For example, note that there is a difference between my own example and these others. In my example – as I was careful to put it – I *have* some spare A and you *have* some extra B; whereas, in the others, it is assumed, if not stated, both that the parties are the *rightful owners* of the things (objects or services) they exchange and that they own those things as private property (which, for libertarians, comes to the same thing of course). The point here is that although 'having' includes rightfully owning it is wider than the latter. To have a thing, in my sense, one need only be in a position to exert control over it. I have an object if I have just stolen it from you and am now refusing to give it back. I have it if I have just stumbled across it in the street (some money), or in the wilderness (a water supply), and am now denying you access. This means that the simple 'newsvendor'-style examples cannot fulfil the theoretical function libertarianism requires of them – or at least not just by themselves. For the libertarian, the exchange between private owners within a free market is, as I put it earlier, a 'paradigmatic exemplar' of freedom and mutual beneficiality. It is supposed to typify these virtues in a way other types of exchange do not. Against this, though, it seems clear, first, that an exchange can take place once I *control* the A and you *control* the B, that 'owning' of any sort need not enter the story. Second, it is clear that once control has been established, the exchange can be 'free' and 'mutually beneficial', at least in the senses of these phrases to which 'newsvendor' stories draw attention.

Consider these examples. First: I steal your A and refuse to return it unless you first give me your precious B. You don't have to, but you agree to the exchange. Here, there is no question of my rightfully owning your

A and yet the exchange is 'free' in precisely the (possibly somewhat minimal) senses at issue. It is also mutually beneficial in the sense that we are both better off than we were immediately prior to the exchange. (I get your B, and you get your A *back*.) Just to forestall a possible objection, I should add that I am aware that many libertarian readers will be quick to object here that this case differs from 'free market exchange' cases in that, unlike them, it involves coercion (in some sense of that slippery word),[1] so it is important to note that one cannot raise this objection without begging many questions. If the theft of a thing and its subsequent return at a price involves coercion, then isn't the 'privatisation' of a publicly owned utility coercion? Or, can't it be held that the Earth is the rightful common property of all – as the True Levellers thought?[2] So doesn't the private ownership of *anything* involve theft and therefore coercion? To be credible, libertarianism must produce arguments sufficient to convince Levellers, more mainstream socialists and other sceptics that none of this is so, and it seems pretty clear that it cannot do so simply by means of an appeal to features of the two-person exchange itself. Again: Suppose that one party to the exchange is a utility, publicly owned under (what libertarians tend to call) 'collectivist' economic arrangements. For example, the water company agrees to maintain the supply to a given individual for another year in return for a sum of money. Here, it seems almost ridiculous to suppose that the exchange need be any less free or mutually beneficial than it would be if the company were privately owned.

Such considerations cast doubt on the libertarian idea that the 'two-person' exchange between private owners within a free market context is somehow unique in the respects presently at issue, which means that libertarianism must supplement its account of such exchanges if it is to reach its desired conclusion. And that, indeed, is what libertarianism does, most usually with a *moralised* account of capitalist property relations. Within popular, off-the-peg, rhetoric this account frequently takes the form of an invocation of responsibility, which governments are urged to give people more of, or, more threateningly, people are urged to acknowledge and shoulder.[3] Within philosophical theory, the usual – though not the only – libertarian move is to invoke an account of *rights* according to which the unrestricted right to private ownership is a fundamental ('human' or 'natural') right. The two-person exchange between private owners is, therefore, held to be unique in a further sense; that is, in the sense that only this type of exchange is morally untainted by the violation of rights.

I don't believe this for a moment, so let me just note one good reason, the following, for treating this type of move with scepticism. Even if some version of the 'rights-based' account of the market were to turn out to be correct, it would only demonstrate that the free market, being a unique respecter of rights, is *morally superior* to other types of system. It would not follow that it is superior in the degree to which it respects freedom, nor in the degree to which it satisfies wants. I agree with Sir Isaiah Berlin that, 'liberty is liberty, not equality or fairness or justice or culture, or human happiness or a quiet conscience' (1969: 125). Since moral goodness is one thing whereas freedom is another, the arguments I have just raised would seem to be immune to any rights-based objection. And yet, despite (what I should have thought to be) the obvious differences between the two, libertarians have a strange tendency to confuse questions concerning rights with questions concerning freedom.

I shall examine the libertarian invocation of rights more closely in Part II. Of course, if the invisible hand thesis itself were to turn out to be true – if it were really the case that the unrestricted free market supplies the best available route to the increase of wealth and human happiness – that would, I guess, also be a reason for investing it with a certain moral superiority. I shall examine this more closely in Part III.

Chapter 3

Reducibility, freedom, the invisible hand

However, the immediate task is to explore the relation between these three theses.

1 THE REDUCIBILITY THESIS

Rothbard's 'buying a newspaper' story is supposed to illustrate the point that, as he puts it, 'The developed market economy, as complex as the system appears to be on the surface, is *nothing more than* a vast network of voluntary and mutually-agreed upon two-person exchanges' (1973: 40). Likewise, *a propos* the Robinsons, Friedman writes that, 'A working model of a society organised through voluntary exchange *is* a free private enterprise exchange economy – what we have been calling competitive capitalism' (1962: 13).[1] (For 'is', read 'is just'.) According to the reducibility thesis, then, the fully developed market economy is 'nothing more than' (or 'reducible to') the sum or aggregate of its discrete components, the individual bilateral exchanges which actually take place.

Let us be clear about exactly what the reducibility thesis amounts to, beginning with the observation that, 'Complex though it appears, the developed market economy is nothing more than a vast network of two-person exchanges' has a vaguely 'scientific' ring to it. It seems to parallel 'Complex though it appears, the universe is nothing more than a vast array of elementary particles' or 'Complex though it appears, the huge diversity of species is nothing more than the expression of genetic material, randomly selected at the micro-biological level.' But don't be fooled. We are dealing with scientism here, not science. There is, of course, some plain and obvious truth in the claim that the whole is nothing more than, or 'no greater than' the sum of its parts, and that – just as there would be no universe if there were no particles – there could be no market economy if there were no bilateral exchanges. It is also the case that, within economic theory, the concept of the bilateral exchange has considerable explanatory power because, like the random mutation of DNA within evolutionary theory, it suggests a single, comprehensible, underlying order from which an initially baffling range of superficially diverse phenomena can be deduced. But the libertarian's version of reducibility functions in neither of these ways. On the contrary, it is an *ethical* claim.

For the libertarian, the point is that the whole (the fully developed economy) can only be *evaluated* in terms of criteria relevant to the evaluation of the individual parts (the discrete exchanges). Considerations which might arise from, for example, the fact that we are dealing with a 'vast network' rather than the odd, isolated, event are thus ruled out of the moral equation on the grounds that the whole can only have properties that the individual parts also possess. (For a good visual analogue, take the original cover illustration for Hobbes's *Leviathan*, whose artist portrays the state, or 'body politic', as a huge artificial person which exhibits – and can only exhibit, though writ large – the features of the large number of smaller, real, people of which it is composed. Like them, it can have no more than one nose, two ears, a beard, and so on.[2] For the libertarian the market economy is, likewise, just one very big and complicated multi-lateral market exchange.) It ought to be patently clear that if this were right, and if it were also the case that the market exchange is paradigmatic of freedom as libertarians hold, then the freedom thesis – according to which there is something especially freedom-respecting about a free market economy – would clearly follow. If it were paradigmatic of want-satisfaction, so too would the invisible hand thesis follow; because, if two people get what they want at the micro, bilateral, level every time an exchange takes place, then – assuming reducibility – it would have to follow that the whole system, considered at the macro level, functions efficiently to satisfy everyone's wants.

Once its true status has been established, it becomes more apparent that there is something very odd indeed about the reducibility thesis, and I shall return to the point. For the moment, let us just note how reducibility plays a role in the work of libertarianism's most influential present-day philosopher, Robert Nozick. For Nozick, the market exchange epitomises both freedom (it can only take place with the consent of the parties directly involved) and justice (no one's rights are violated), and reducibility comes with a temporal dimension added. The main purpose of the 'Wilt Chamberlain' story is, thus, to illustrate the point that there can be nothing unjust about the outcome of a repetition of exchanges in sequence if there is nothing unjust about any of those exchanges taken individually. Rights (upon which, for Nozick, justice and freedom hang) are passed, as it were, from hand to hand, like the baton in a relay race, and, as he rhetorically asks, 'If D_1 was a just distribution, and people voluntarily moved from it to D_2 . . . isn't D_2 also just?' (1974: 161). For an example of the way this type of argument can come to play a role as propaganda in the wider world, we need only turn to Sir Keith Joseph and Jonathan Sumption's book, *Equality*, which contains a passage which is almost identical to Nozick's. Only the characters are changed, rendering them more accept-able to a certain up-market taste. A 'celebrated conductor', one 'Gerbert von Charabanc', is substituted for Wilt Chamberlain. Sir Keith and his co-author invite us to draw a conclusion corresponding to Nozick's, the conclusion that 'Since inequality arises from the operation of innumerable preferences, it cannot be evil unless those preferences are themselves evil' (1979: 78).

2   REDUCIBILITY AND FREEDOM

The libertarian thesis under consideration rests upon an *a priori* appeal to reason. In other words, it does not base its conclusions upon observation or historical fact. Rather it holds that they flow logically from an abstrac-tion: an ideal model of the 'pure' free market at work. That is absolutely as it should be, and the case against libertarianism which, as from now, I shall begin to outline also rests upon an *a priori* appeal to the same ideal model. The core of my argument will be that an accurate appraisal of that model shows that it logically entails conclusions quite contrary to those libertarians would like us to draw.

2.1   The 'quasi-Lockean scenario'

Just to get a focus on this, consider the *quasi-Lockean scenario* ('quasi'-Lock-ean because there are, no doubt, differences between it and Locke's own well-known account of the transition from an initial situation in which the Earth is commonly owned to a fully developed economic system based on private property; also because it is unnecessary to address tangled ques-tions about exactly how to interpret Locke here.)[3]

> *Stage one* Humans are created, fully grown and hungry, and more or less evenly spaced across the surface of the Earth. They need food and shelter, but plenty and abundance reign and there is consequently no need for anyone who is at least averagely industrious to starve or go short. Nevertheless, it is also the case that people must work on raw nature if they are to survive, transforming it to meet their needs. This

they proceed to do. As they work, they establish possession over those parts of the world upon which they have laboured, and, pretty soon, some individuals have managed to create more of certain things than they personally need. However, those same individuals also lack other things and, as a result, 'two-person, mutually beneficial, market exchanges' begin to take place.

Stage two The process initiated at stage one has finally culminated in the development of a fully-fledged capitalist economy. Some individuals have proved more industrious and enterprising than others, some have been luckier and, as a result of such factors, inequalities of wealth have grown up. These are compounded over generations by inheritance. Eventually, the stock of 'raw nature' available for acquisition has dried up and a proletariat has emerged with nothing to sell but its own labour.

As we have seen, libertarians hold that there is nothing morally objectionable about the bilateral exchanges which take place at stage one. I agree (with reservations). They must also hold – in line with the reducibility thesis – that there can therefore be nothing at all objectionable about the situation which has developed by the time stage two is reached. I disagree.

Let us consider this more closely, taking stage one first. For a start, there is the fact that, unlike Locke, who writes of labour that 'being the unquestionable property of the labourer, no man but he can have a right to what that is once joined to' (1988: 288), or Nozick, whose entire theory is premised on the assertion that 'Individuals have rights, and there are things no person or group may do to them (without violating their rights)' (1974: ix), I can see no reason for invoking the notion of a natural ('human' or 'fundamental') *right* to property at this stage, nor any of the complicated metaphysical paraphernalia which tends to go with it. I prefer to rely upon what I take to be a fairly uncontroversial precept of common morality according to which, even where there is nothing especially morally praiseworthy about a person's having or doing some thing (reading trashy romantic fiction, jogging round the park, eating too much ice-cream, you name it) *there is no reason why he or she should not have or do it if there is no countervailing moral consideration to be taken into account*; where 'all other things are equal' in other words. It seems clear that persons who have established possession over things at stage one satisfy just this condition. The crucial feature here is – obviously – abundance; a small population relative to resources. This is quite sufficient to justify a person's establishing possession, in the simple sense of *control*, over a thing because it makes it highly unlikely that he or she will have disadvantaged anyone else in the process of acquisition. As Locke himself puts it, 'he that leaves as much as another can make use of, does as good as take nothing at all' (1988: 291). I should add that, where someone who exerts control over a thing is also the person who created (or helped create) it, a further presumption in favour of his or her continuing to keep it seems to me to come into play. But this is also in line with what I take to be a perfectly ordinary precept of common morality, according to which the creator of a thing does have *some sort* of claim over it, and I can see no justification whatsoever for inflating it into a story about natural rights. (There are also other possible justifications for the precept. For example, it might be argued that persons with their own lives to lead, and who therefore need to plan, need to have certain expectations respected by others.)

So, although I agree with libertarians that there is nothing to object to in the possession of things by 'private' individuals at stage one, or in the bilateral exchanges which result, my reasons for thinking so are different. The same goes for the status of third parties. Note that, for any bilateral exchange between persons P_1 and P_2, there is at least one other person, P_3 (and, in addition to P_3, everyone else in the world), who is not directly involved in the exchange and who consequently does not consent to its taking place. But, at stage one, where the exchange can be pictured as an isolated event with no discernible effect on P_3's welfare, the fact can be discounted as of no moral consequence. There is also the practical consideration that 'If such a consent as that was necessary, Man had starved, notwithstanding the Plenty God had given him' (1988: 288). Similar considerations apply to the fact that, as a result of the exchange, a possibility is *foreclosed* to P_3. For example, suppose that P_1 sells P_2 a field. There is now something P_3 could have had (or have done) and which he or she can no longer have (or do), namely possess or gain access to the field, and P_3 (together with everyone else) is strictly speaking, although in an insignificant respect, 'worse off'. This is insignificant because, in conditions of plenty (e.g. where the field is a tiny portion of a vast prairie) it is difficult to see how P_3 (or anyone else) could have reasonable cause for complaint.

But the reasons I have just given for discounting the consent of, and the opportunities open to, third parties at stage one are, as before, contingent upon features peculiar to that stage, principally abundance. The reasons may cease to apply where conditions change. My view is therefore quite different from that of libertarians such as Nozick who insist on portraying transfers of property as simultaneously involving the transfer of fundamental rights (as if the money you pass over in exchange for the newspaper were like holy water, mysteriously imbued with some awesome moral essence). For Nozick, as we have seen, a just arrangement is nothing more than the outcome of repeated, direct and 'face-to-face' exchanges between individuals who have an 'entitlement' to 'hold' the things they exchange.[4] On such a view, there are no circumstances under which third parties can be consistently granted full consideration.

The broad outline of the case I am about to make should be discernible by now. It is that factors which are of no moral significance at stage one acquire a great deal of significance by the time stage two is reached. At stage two, circumstances have changed and we are confronted with a fully developed capitalist economy in which bilateral exchanges between consenting individuals normally *do* have far-reaching, and often deleterious, consequences for third parties not directly involved. At stage two, the foreclosure of opportunities to those third parties renders them worse off in a morally significant, not just a logically nit-picking, sense. This means, for example, that the consent (or potential consent) of third parties must almost certainly enter the moral equation at stage two. The fact that you or I have certainly not consented to the specific pattern of distribution which has resulted from the constant repetition of two-person exchanges is (or, maybe, should be) of importance to us in a way it would not be if we were the isolated inhabitants of a state of nature. In a modern state there are, moreover, many methods available for obtaining that consent – the use of democratic procedures, for example. Imperfect though these may be, there is no need to swallow the improbable libertarian myth according to which they are far *worse* respecters of choice than the market left to itself.

This conclusion contradicts the reducibility thesis, of course, for it states that criteria irrelevant to the assessment of the discrete parts, each taken singly, become relevant to the evaluation of the whole, considered as a 'vast network'. Note that one way to deny it (perhaps the only way) is to insist, once again, upon the existence of fundamental property rights acquired at stage one. The main criterion for the assessment of the whole would then be that property rights are respected throughout, at both stages. But, as I shall argue later, these do not exist, and without the assumption of such rights the conclusion I have just drawn is in a way obvious. Incidentally, note also that I have not found it necessary to invent some nebulous supra-entity with suspect totalitarian or fascistic credentials in order to reach my conclusion. My argument states, on the contrary, that factors which are *latent*, though insignificant, at the micro level (stage one) *emerge* into significance at the macro level (stage two). Nozick again:

> But there is no *social entity* with a good that undergoes some sacrifice for its own good. There are only individual people, different individual

people, with their own individual lives. Using one of these people for
the benefit of others, uses him and benefits the others. Nothing more.

(1974: 33)

Construed as a statement of moral principle, 'There are only individual
people' and so on, is fine. Like Nozick, I take it as a datum that every
person has his or her life to lead. (His or her *own* life, that is.) But construed
as an axiom of the reducibility thesis, with the implication that only an
unfettered free market can respect the moral datum, the remark is deeply
misguided. Nozick is wrong to suggest that critics of his position need to
invent a mythical 'social entity', and the Right have been allowed to get
away with this kind of easy insinuation for far too long. (As for Nozick's
talk of 'using people' and 'sacrifice', with its connotations of blood and
death, to describe such activities as taxing the rich, I reserve comment.)

2.2 The freedom thesis

Let us now go on to explore the implications of the foregoing case a little
further, this time with special reference to libertarian claims concerning
freedom. Libertarians believe that the market is a great respecter of
individual freedom, more so than any other conceivable 'systems' or sets
of arrangements. I shall now argue against this that, for the typical or
'representative' individual, A, there is no more reason for thinking that 'A
is free' is more likely to be true where the free market prevails than there
is where it does not. As I shall stress, this conclusion holds for those senses
of 'freedom' which *libertarians themselves* endorse.

But first, a word of caution. So far as their reactions to the arguments I
am about to present are concerned, it seems to me that readers are likely
to fall into one or the other of two groups. On the one hand, there will be
those who are not especially familiar with the intricacies of the philosophical debate surrounding this subject. I should warn members of this group
that what I am about to say is likely to strike them as plain obvious. Some
may find it so obvious that they will wonder why I am wasting my time
saying it, and they may well be surprised to learn that there is a strong
consensus of mainstream philosophical opinion according to which the
case I am about to make is too pathetically naive to be taken seriously. The
former group is right – the conclusions I draw here *are* obvious – and it
really would be a waste of time spelling them out if it were not for the
existence of the latter; i.e. those who share in the philosophical consensus.
This raises some interesting questions: how is it that philosophy has
become so introvertedly self-mesmerised that so many philosophers can

so confidently deny the obvious? Or is it just laziness?

Before facing these questions, let us consider definitions of 'freedom' popular with libertarians. There are three in particular. First, libertarians are fond of insisting that 'freedom' denotes a concept which is essentially 'negative' in character. By this they mean to stress that there is nothing fancy about freedom; that individual freedom is essentially a simple matter of there being actions available to an individual which that individual would not be prevented from doing were he or she to try. In support of this, libertarians frequently cite Sir Isaiah Berlin as an authority (although Berlin is not, I think, himself a libertarian). In a famous sentence, Berlin puts it this way:

> If I am prevented by others from doing what I could otherwise do, I am to that degree unfree.
>
> (1958: 122)

Second, libertarians tend to claim that freedom is the absence of subjection to the will (sometimes the 'arbitrary' will) of another person or persons. Third, and more specifically, they tend to define freedom as the absence of coercion. These second and third definitions of 'freedom' are distinct, though clearly related, and libertarians have a tendency to run them together. The following, also fairly well-known, passages from Hayek's *The Constitution of Liberty* illustrate the point.

> It [freedom] has meant always the possibility of a person's acting according to his own decisions and plans, in contrast to the position of one who was irrevocably subject to the will of another; who by arbitrary decision could coerce him to act or not to act in specific ways. The time honoured phrase by which this freedom has often been described is therefore 'independence of the arbitrary will of another'.
>
> (1960: 12)

> 'freedom' refers solely to a relation of men to other men, and the only infringement on it is coercion by men.[5]
>
> (1960: 12)

I strongly sympathise with the sentiment that a philosophical account of freedom should be kept realistic and down to earth, uncluttered by fancy metaphysical junk. I also agree that a person lacks freedom if he or she is prevented by others from doing what he or she could otherwise do, if he or she is 'subject to the will of another', or if he or she is coerced by another (though whether any of these, taken singly or in some combination, amounts to a *definition* of 'freedom' is another question). The question at issue here, however, is whether it can be *any more true* of the pure free market that it respects freedom, defined in terms of the absence of such factors, than it can be true of other conceivable systems. It is, I think, a fairly straightforward matter to demonstrate that it cannot.

For example – first – take the fact that a fully developed market economy requires an equally developed legal system, both to define spheres of private ownership and to ensure that those spheres are protected. Individuals are thus permitted to do certain things and prevented from doing others. Where you and I are the private owners of our respective refrigerators, for example, the law permits me to take groceries from my own refrigerator as I like, whereas it would punish me for strolling into your kitchen and taking groceries from yours. You could have me arrested for even trying. But this does nothing much to distinguish a market system based on individual private ownership from others, because other conceivable systems simply permit and prevent differently. Suppose, alternatively, that you and I are the joint owners of one big refrigerator. (We live under 'collectivist' arrangements or maybe we are just married to each other.) I can now remove groceries from the refrigerator just as you can – although there may be rules specifying just how many – and either of us can be arrested for trying to stop the other from doing so. What this means is that if freedom is a matter of there being available actions which one would be prevented from doing were one to try, as Berlin maintains it is, then there is nothing to distinguish capitalism from 'collectivism' in this respect. It can be no more true of the market that it respects freedom *in this sense of 'freedom'* than it can be of other conceivable possibilities.

Second, there is the fact that a developed market economy – and a 'pure' market economy in particular – will contain *inequalities* of wealth. As we have seen, the quasi-Lockean scenario portrays these as developing from differences between individuals in skill and luck. The existence of such natural differences is so clearly inescapable that it has to be taken into account, and it is certainly difficult to see how inheritance could not reinforce the inequalities, as they develop, pretty rapidly. To pre-empt a possible misunderstanding, let me stress here that inequality *itself* is not the central issue so far as this part of my argument is concerned. Reasonable people of moral sensitivity (and much windy rhetoric on 'the politics of envy', etc., notwithstanding) will find more than a certain degree of inequality objectionable, and only libertarians will demur. But the point at issue is not that.[6] It is, rather, that inequalities of wealth tend to bring inequalities of power in their wake and, as a consequence, to compromise *freedom.*[7]

Again, it seems fairly obvious. If you are the private owner of the factory in which I must work if I am to have any hope of a decent life, then you have power over me; to employ me or not, to determine my working conditions, my rate of pay, and so on. Again, if we both want to buy the same house or flat, but you are richer than me – rich enough, maybe, to price me out of the housing market altogether – then you exert power over me when you make your higher bid. In these cases, your power gives you the potential to act in a way which causes me to suffer, and I am thus, in a fairly obvious sense of the phrase, 'subject to your will'. So if freedom is, as Hayek thinks, the absence of subjection to the will of another then it is a false assertion that the market, unlike other systems, respects freedom in Hayek's sense, just as it is in Berlin's.

Third, as for coercion, the anti-libertarian case seems, if anything, still more clear. *Any* conceivable legal system requires coercion to hold it in place. A law is a sort of threat: 'Do this, don't do that, or you will be punished'. It is a commonplace of legal theory that this is so, as it is also a commonplace that coercion is essentially a question of the use of threats and force to manipulate others. Since a legal system designed to define and protect private property will, like any other, require the usual array of police, courts, prisons, and so on, it has to be false that a pure free market is uniquely characterised by the absence of coercion.

But libertarianism is not monolithic or all of a piece, and only some libertarians would deny the point. (Rothbard is an example.) An alternative move is to try to marginalise or neutralise it by insisting that capitalist coercion is somehow different. For example, Hayek writes that

> Coercion, however, cannot be altogether avoided because the only way to avoid it is by the threat of coercion. Free society has met this problem by conferring the monopoly of coercion on the state and by attempting to limit this power of the state to instances where it is required to prevent coercion by private persons. This is possible only by protecting known private spheres of the individuals against interference by others and delimiting these private spheres, not by specific assignation, but by creating conditions under which the individual can determine his own sphere by relying on rules which tell him what the government will do in different types of situations.

> (1960: 21)

The passage merits a couple of passing comments, namely first that although it is, of course, desirable that a government should, as Hayek adds, be 'made impersonal and dependent upon general, abstract rules', so that 'even the coercive acts of government become data on which the individual can base his own plans' (ibid.), none of this does anything to distinguish the society within which a free market operates from other possibilities. The key notions here are openness and predictability, but there is absolutely no good reason for thinking that a social democratic or socialist government must be closed and unpredictable (or, for that matter, that a capitalist government will not be). Second, that said, however, it is noticeable that Hayek's remark contains a certain anti-democratic streak, for it is commonly held that one great virtue of democracy is that it permits changes of government. For example, there is nothing wildly radical about Karl Popper's argument that this is its greatest virtue, that democracy supplies 'governments of which we can get rid without bloodshed' because 'the social institutions provide means by which the rulers may be dismissed by the ruled' (1945, I: 124). But – of course – where governments can change, so can the rules, and democracy must therefore contain an inherent element of unpredictability. Popper's comment occurs in the context of a critique of Plato (whom he regards as the arch-totalitarian). I don't find it too surprising that Hayek, in contrast to Popper and like Plato, should have advocated immovable rule by those who are old and set-in-their ways; a 'democracy' containing 'an assembly containing persons between their forty-fifth and their sixtieth year', these being 'elected, for instance, for 15 years and one-fifteenth of their number being replaced every year'. Hayek adds

> It would further seem to me expedient to provide that at each election the representatives should be chosen by and from only one age group so that every citizen would vote only once in his life, say in his forty-fifth year, for a representative chosen from his age group.
>
> (1978: 117)[8]

Some democracy! The observation is tangential to the point, however, because the point is simply this: since, as Hayek says, 'coercion . . . cannot be altogether avoided' (ibid.: 21), even where free market conditions prevail, it has to be *false* that a free market system is uniquely characterised by the absence of coercion. The general conclusion for which I have been arguing – that the libertarian's freedom thesis is false, even for those senses of 'freedom' which libertarians themselves tend to favour – also follows.

2.3 An invocation of authority

I think the reader will agree that the anti-libertarian case I have just outlined is fairly straightforward. It isn't difficult to think of different types of legal system as specifying differing patterns of freedom and unfreedom, or to see that capitalism requires a police force for its continued existence. Moreover, I can hardly be said to have been expecting the reader to follow an abstruse and detailed chain of reasoning through or to grasp difficult concepts drawn from within, say, economic theory. So, what of the question to which I alluded earlier? How is it that a sizeable portion of the philosophical establishment has become so adept at denying the obvious that it is even capable of dismissing out of hand something as simple and straightforward as the position I take here as not just wrong but naive?

The answer has a lot to do with the enormous influence wielded by Sir Isaiah Berlin's essay, 'Two Concepts of Liberty', which first appeared in 1958. Since then, it has acquired a sort of biblical status; so much so that philosophers and others who should be spending their time thinking have tended, instead, to rely upon its authority, believing it sufficient to lazily reiterate or gesticulate in the direction of the claims Berlin makes. The following example – one of many – is taken from Joseph and Sumption's book.

> If one examines carefully the concept of freedom as 'freedom to' it becomes increasingly difficult to regard it as freedom at all. A person who is unable to do something which he would like to do may be unfree but is not necessarily so. As Sir Isaiah Berlin pointed out in a memorable essay, it all depends on the reason why he cannot do it. If the reason is that some other person, or group of persons is intentionally preventing him from doing it, then he is to that extent unfree. But he is not unfree if he is not capable of achieving it because of some lack of capacity in himself. 'It is not lack of freedom to be unable to fly like an eagle or swim like a whale', said Helvetius. It is not lack of freedom to be unable to write a poem in Latin hexameters or play bridge or make money in business. Poverty is one kind of personal incapacity. But it is not coercion. The possession of the money one would like is not the same thing as liberty, simply because both of them are desirable.

(1979: 48)

Sumption and Sir Keith haven't really subjected the concept of freedom to a careful examination, of course. They are simply playing the parrot to Berlin's Long John Silver. To see how their position differs from my own, notice how they focus upon such factors as 'intentional prevention' and so attempt to restrict the concepts of freedom and coercion to direct and, so to speak, 'face-to-face' interchanges between individuals. Their approach is thus in line with the reducibility thesis, and its thrust is therefore directly antithetical to that of my own argument, according to which the liberty-compromising aspects of the market system are to be found less in details, internal to the typical face-to-face market transaction, and more in general features which arise at the macro level as the constant repetition of bilateral exchanges progresses. By contrast, Joseph and Sumption deny that the general features can count as freedom restricting. To illustrate the point: according to me, I am 'subject to your will', and therefore unfree, when you price me out of the housing market with your higher bid *even where we are each unaware of the other's existence*. In my view, my freedom is compromised by you because we are both participants in the same market system. We are both, if you like, swimmers in the same pool. Joseph and Sumption (and Berlin) would argue against this that, since you neither intentionally prevent me from buying the house nor directly coerce me into withdrawing my offer, it cannot *make sense* to say that my freedom is limited by you.

Not that there isn't something to be said for some of the positions Joseph and Sumption take. For example, I think they are right to stress that 'It is not lack of freedom to be unable to write a poem in Latin hexameters'. But they are mostly wrong, and if one really 'examines carefully the concept of freedom' it becomes clear that Berlin's analysis adds up to a series of *non sequiturs* and misleading distortions. (See Chapter 5.)

3 RAISING THE SPECTRE OF 'COLLECTIVISM'

Let me summarise: for any typically placed[9] individual (person A) certain otherwise available courses of action will be closed off by preventing obstacles. That individual will be subject to the wills of others in certain respects, and liable to certain forms of coercion. However, there will also be actions available to person A, and respects in which he or she is autonomous and uncoerced. Therefore, he or she will be unfree in certain respects but free in others. The difference between free market arrangements and most others (socialist or welfare state arrangements, for example) is such that the former's presence or absence has no bearing on the truth or falsity of 'A is free'; at least, not for the senses of 'free' libertarians tend to stress. This is the conclusion to be drawn from the argument I have so far developed.

But we must now consider an objection according to which this conclusion completely misses the point. The objection concedes that the free market rests on coercion, as other systems do, but points out that simply stressing the fact fails to acknowledge that coercion admits of degrees – from trivial to serious. It is true enough, or so it runs, that, if you should feel inclined to do so, you will be coerced into not helping yourself to the contents of your neighbour's refrigerator by laws designed to protect private property. But, or so it continues, had you lived elsewhere you might have found yourself spending years in the gulag as a slave. You might have remained there for fear of the violent death you would have risked had you tried to escape. That would have been coercion too, and wouldn't it have been worse – *much* worse – than the sort of coercion experienced by anyone under free market conditions? To put it another way, don't other systems require *more serious* violations of liberty?

Most libertarians tend to argue that they do; more specifically that the only alternative to a pure free market economy is an extreme form of totalitarianism often labelled 'collectivism'. What is meant by 'collectivism', then? Hayek's *The Road to Serfdom* is the most celebrated exposition of this either/or thesis, and the following phrases, culled from the pages of the book, will give something of 'collectivism's' flavour: the 'collective and "conscious" direction of all social forces to deliberately chosen goals'; the 'regimentation of economic life'; 'the central direction of all economic activity according to a single plan, laying down how the resources of society should be "consciously directed" to serve particular ends in a definite way'; 'the direction of all our activities to a single plan'; 'the deliberate organisation of the labours of society for a definite social goal' (1944: 15, 25, 26, 42). According to Hayek, even the most timid step in the direction of state intervention in the market, or towards the redistribution of income, inevitably places one at the top of the slippery slope which leads to the totalitarian abyss. As he says

> Few are ready to recognise that the rise of Fascism and Nazism was not a reaction against the socialist trends of the preceding period, but a necessary outcome of those tendencies
>
> (1944: 3)

So, 'collectivism' conjures up images of Hitler's Germany and Stalin's Russia. Collectivism involves a sort of militarisation of the whole of society, under which, in the worst cases, every single aspect of the individual's life is regulated by a central authority. Civil liberties are out of the question. And throughout *The Road to Serfdom* 'collectivism' is contrasted with such phenomena as 'the spontaneous and uncontrolled efforts of individuals', 'the free exercise of human ingenuity', 'the spontaneous forces found in a free society' and 'the impersonal and anonymous mechanism of the market' (1944: 11, 12, 15). In short, you have a choice, or so it is alleged: the sunny uplands of spontaneity and freedom (capitalism) or the dark nightmare, the jackboot grinding the human face forever ('collectivism'). Can this really be true, or is it an hysterical and exaggerated claim? Either way, it is important to give it a fair run for its money and the way to do that is to bear in mind throughout that the only manifestations of coercion and force which need concern us are those required by the ideal model. This means, for a start, that appeals to the historical record are beside the point. For example, it would be all too tempting to try to argue against Hayek by pointing out that history supplies numerous examples of capitalist economies existing contemporaneously with brutal totalitarian regimes (Hitler's Germany, Salazar's Portugal, Pinochet's Chile, much of the Middle East, and so on), but the open-minded stance requires the assumption that, until things have been proven otherwise, the explanation for the nature of the regime has nothing to do with the nature of the prevailing economic arrangements in these cases. Likewise, supporters of the either/or thesis need to show, not just that socialism, 'welfare statist' redistributivism or anything else which might count as non-capitalism have gone hand-in-hand with totalitarianism at various times, but that socialism *requires* suppression and brutality – 'serious' coercion, in other words – for its preservation. (If the historical record were unambiguous, that might be a different matter. If history showed that socialism had always gone together with totalitarianism and that capitalism never had, we might then have good cause to go seeking reasons for this. But, in fact, the record is quite unclear; and, in a century in which events have, for the most part, been dominated by the existence of two great power blocs, each espousing a different side of this pair of ideologies, there is also the muddying effect of the influence each has exerted on the other to consider.)

As we have seen, the ideal model of the free market demands that force will be required to hold its structure in place; that is, to protect the spheres of private ownership which must exist if it is to function. Likewise, a socialist set-up will no doubt require some use of coercive force to protect the rights of ownership, the rights of control, and the redistributive rules necessary for its function. The question is, *how much* force will be required to hold these differing structures in place? The answer to that is simply that *it all depends*. For any system, the degree of force required to maintain it will be a function of two groups of factors: its structural features on the one hand and, on the other, features of the specific situation in which the attempt to maintain it is being made. For example, there is the question of how generally popular capitalism or socialism happen to be at a given time. It was obviously far easier to introduce socialist measures in Britain in 1945 (when there was a landslide electoral victory for a Labour government with a sweeping programme of nationalisation) than it would have been in 1979 (when Thatcher came to power). It would have been difficult to introduce anything *other* than socialism into Russia in 1917, and much the same would have gone for Cuba in 1959. At any rate, that is what it seems to me to be reasonable to assume and there is a complete absence of good reasons for assuming otherwise. Capitalism and socialism seem to be in the same boat.

And yet Hayek holds that, whereas the former respects freedom the latter must lead to totalitarianism (this being 'a necessary outcome'). How? Hayek's argument is helped by a certain rhetorical redefinition. Socialism is in effect equated with the direction of all social forces to deliberately chosen goals and thus with the worst form of centralised authoritarianism. But there is no good reason to make the connection. (Note also the connotations of 'collectivism'. Hayek's choice of word creates the association between socialism and totalitarianism, but not with an argument. As with the *Saturday Evening Post* stuff, and the 'scientific' flavour with which libertarians sometimes spice their formulations of the reducibility thesis, there is a sort of deadpan rhetoric at work here.)

The question his argument really raises is that of how the existence of liberal institutions can affect an attempt to impose or establish an economic order, so let us briefly consider this. Libertarians frequently describe their doctrine as a form of liberalism – it is, according to some, the only true liberalism – but this is wrong. The two are completely different. Libertarianism is market worship whereas liberalism is the view of the world characterised as follows by the foremost contemporary liberal philosopher, John Rawls:[10]

> One task of liberalism as a political doctrine is to answer the question: how is social unity to be understood, given that there can be no public agreement on the one rational good, and a plurality of opposing and incommensurable conceptions must be taken as given? And granted that social unity is conceivable in some definite way, under what conditions is it actually possible?
>
> (1985: 249)

The task of liberal institutions is thus to supply those conditions in the form, for example, of the democratic conditions which, as Popper sees it, permit peaceful changes of government. Liberal institutions can act as 'checks and balances', as 'side-constraints' on attempts to impose any economic order. (For example, if they work they will prohibit slavery.) Capitalist demagogues can overstep the side-constraints, as can demagogues imbued with some form of 'collectivist' vision, but there is no reason whatsoever for believing that the side-constraints cannot serve equally well to moderate both, including attempts to introduce a welfare state and public ownership of major industries in line with ideals of equality and community. So, it seems that the Reds under Hayek's bed are herrings, and that his claim that we must choose between 'the extreme decentralisation of free competition' and 'the complete centralisation of a single plan' (Hayek 1944: 31) is without foundation.

I should add that it wouldn't help Hayek at all to introduce the notion of a tendency here. In 1973 Hayek wrote, of the 'collectivist tendencies' he had discerned in 1944, that 'I did not, as many misunderstood me, contend that if government interfered at all with economic affairs it was bound to go the whole way to a totalitarian system' (1978: 105). Given that he had previously described the latter as a necessary outcome of the former, it isn't surprising that he should have been misunderstood. On the contrary, this looks like a retraction. But, in any case, unless one shares the biblical sentiment according to which 'whoever looketh on a woman to lust after her hath committed adultery with her already in his heart' (St Matthew 5: 27–8) – i.e. unless one thinks that having a tendency to do some evil thing is just as bad as actually doing it – then it is difficult to see how Hayek's argument could be helped by this. Those who seek power, being the sort of people they often are, will of course exhibit a tendency to increase their power. They will exhibit, if you like, a tendency to totalitarianism, but the liberal institutions are there to stop them doing that. Hayek offers no good reason for thinking that they must necessarily fail, which is what he needs.

Such manoeuvres help mask the simple truth that there is no special relation between capitalism and 'free' liberal institutions, any more than there is a necessary relation between socialism and totalitarian slavery. Finally, libertarians sometimes maintain that capitalism avoids the totalitarian nightmare by spreading power widely. 'So long as property is divided among many owners, none of them acting independently has exclusive power to determine the income and position of particular people' (Hayek 1944: 77–8). This denies the obvious fact, already noted in our discussion of the quasi-Lockean scenario, that it does no such thing. Otherwise, the hypothesis that capitalism, or governments sympathetic to free market ideas, will use the degree and type of coercion required to maintain the system in place, appears to hold. Consider:

> But the Public Order Act of 1986, the first major public order statute for fifty years, has made sure that the right to demonstrate openly can be seriously restricted and controlled. . . . It extends existing controls over processions and marches, it creates for the first time in the history of our law statutory controls over open-air meetings and picketing, it creates a new range of widely drawn public order offences, and it devises the first statutory offence of criminal trespass. Above all it gives the police, in the exercise of all these powers, an almost unchallengeable discretion, described by the Prime Minister in a speech to the Conservative Party conference as a 'blank cheque'.
>
> (Thornton 1989: 35–6)

Or

> One private organisation, the Economic League, provides a blacklisting service to more than 2,000 British firms. It keeps secret files on allegedly subversive workers, alleging links with left-wing political groups or radical causes such as CND or feminism, or trade union activity such as taking part in a strike or sit-in. This information is obtained from subscribing companies, newspaper cuttings and other sources of information including paid informers. . . . A Granada World in Action television programme in February 1987 demonstrated that people on the blacklist could be deprived of employment. . . . A complaint by the Economic League that the programme was unjust and unfair was later rejected by the Broadcasting Complaints Commission.
>
> (ibid.: 27)

The aspects of Thatcherism suggestive of a 'police state' may have lacked Stalin's grandeur of scale, but the comparison is otherwise apt. From a whole list, carefully itemised and categorised by Peter Thornton in his *Decade of Decline*, I have chosen these two in particular to illustrate the point that one cannot object to either the 1986 Public Order Act or to the activities of the Economic League on libertarian grounds alone. The former would have been drawn up with the events of the 1984–5 miners' strike much in mind, of course, and it specifically curtails the right to picket to the bare minimum (two at the back gate of the factory, two at the front gate and two at the side gate). To give the police *carte blanche* in the control of industrial disputes is, perhaps, no more than to introduce the minimum force necessary to ensure that the ground rules the market requires for its operation are observed. Likewise, it is difficult to see how a libertarian could think of the Economic League (a sort of privatised secret police) as anything more than a commercial undertaking legitimately purveying its wares to other commercial undertakings who, presumably, have a 'right to know' certain facts about potential employees.

Contra Friedman, according to whom 'History suggests only that capitalism is a necessary condition for political freedom' (1962: 10), history suggests nothing of the sort and philosophy suggests that, in certain conditions at least, the preservation of the former is both necessary and sufficient to ensure the denial of the latter. If civil liberties have survived the Thatcher years at all, it is not libertarianism we have to thank.

4 REDUCIBILITY AND THE INVISIBLE HAND

Libertarians attach a great deal of importance to the invisible hand thesis and consequently offer quite a number of arguments in its support. For the moment, I shall confine myself to pointing out that it requires a certain artifice to reconcile that thesis with the reducibility claim.

As the reader will recall, the invisible hand thesis states that the free market mechanism is the most efficient there is for ensuring the satisfaction of human needs, desires, preferences, and so on; 'wants' for short. Of course, this conclusion can only be logically derived from the reducibility thesis as a strict corollary with the help of the assumption that the bilateral market exchange is a paradigmatic exemplar of want satisfaction. This is questionable to say the least, on the grounds that it ignores the possibility that a person may have nothing to exchange, and so no means with which to satisfy a given want. It also ignores the possibility that third parties, not directly involved in the exchange, may have wants which are not satisfied – or are even frustrated – as a result of the exchanges which do take place. If you like, the thesis falsely equates 'demand' with 'effective demand'.

But, even with the above assumption, we should first note that it seems a fairly simple matter to think of examples of wants which do not seem to be satisfied within the context of a fully developed free market economy (stage two of the quasi-Lockean scenario). For example, there is the possibility that a person might want the economic system prevailing within his or her own country not to be based upon free market principles. The very existence of the system would appear to frustrate the want in question and so falsify the invisible hand thesis. Nor is this possibility 'academic', nor 'merely logical'. The majority of British voters at the 1992 general election shared this particular want, or at least they wanted not to live under the 'pure' free market arrangements libertarians advocate. Likewise, one can assume that the voters who repeatedly return social democratic governments to power in many Western European countries share a certain scepticism of the invisible hand, and that they do not want to be ruled by it.

Moreover, the possibility of this want being unsatisfied by the market opens up the same possibility for other wants too. For example, it is safe to assume that, of the thousands who spend the freezing London nights sleeping in cardboard boxes, the majority do not want to spend the night that way. They want to sleep somewhere else tomorrow night. People want clean air and a healthy environment. From what private individual or company are they to buy these things? People want open spaces and a coastline freely available to all. I want my child to be educated in a well-resourced school within the context of a public education system informed by an egalitarian, democratic ideal. Isn't this ruled out by a privately based system which treats inequality as of no consequence? It isn't at all obvious that the market can do anything much to cater for such wants as these. Perhaps there is, after all, some argument to show that, despite appearances, it can – or at least to show, more modestly, that the market does better even if it isn't perfect – but it has to be admitted that there are some pretty good reasons for scepticism.

How is the libertarian to answer this? Well, here is how Sir Keith and his co-author do it.

> No man can regard himself objectively. He cannot treat himself as the equal of every other man. He cannot put his own desires, which he experiences at first hand, after those of others which he observes at second or third hand. He cannot subordinate his own interests to those of others. If one allows for a handful of saints and ascetics, men have always put themselves first.
>
> (1979: 119)

The argument is correct, of course. Who could disagree with Sir Keith that the market is capable of satisfying all wants with the exception of those wants which it is not capable of satisfying? The rhetorical strategy is not too nice. Sir Keith's rule is, first, to rule out the second category of wants on the grounds that they are not 'real' or 'genuine' and, second, to call those who have them names, weirdos, freaks, hippies, or, as Sir Keith sums them up, 'a handful of saints and ascetics'. If you don't take these people seriously – and 'these people' amount to anyone with a want which cannot be supplied by the market – then you can make the invisible hand thesis true by definition. However, and as Sir Keith would no doubt agree, everything has a price. The cost of saving the invisible hand thesis this way is that it reduces it to an uninformative, philosophically pusillanimous, tautology.

Chapter 4

Market romances II
Love is strange

I should now like to examine the relation between the reducibility thesis and the invisible hand thesis more closely. Not all libertarians seek to derive the latter from the former,[1] but each is foundational to libertarianism in the sense that each is supposed to support important claims. Without the former, it would be impossible for the libertarian to argue that there can be nothing morally objectionable about the outcome of a repetition of morally innocent bilateral exchanges across time. Libertarianism would then be forced to abandon the moral high ground it claims in the stance it takes against intervention with the market. Without the latter, it would clearly forsake a different argument against such intervention. A libertarianism forced to abandon one or the other would be seriously weakened. This is very unfortunate for libertarianism, because the two theses stand in logical contradiction to each other. Let us begin by exploring this.

1 A LOGICAL DILEMMA

I shall take the reducibility thesis first. As the reader will recall, this is an ethical claim according to which the whole can only be evaluated in terms of criteria relevant to the evaluation of its individual components. What I have to say here is relevant to all versions of reducibility of which I am aware. I shall use Joseph and Sumption's formulation as an example, if only for its blunt clarity (there is also something touching about the breathless innocence and enthusiasm with which they endorse it). To recap, this is how they formulate the thesis.

> Since inequality arises from the operation of innumerable preferences, it cannot be evil unless those preferences are themselves evil.
>
> (1979: 78)

So, why should we believe this? It is noticeable that Joseph and Sumption's conclusion is announced more or less *ex cathedra*. *Equality* contains no close analysis of ethical concepts, for example, and its writers do not appear to have done any serious empirical work on the psychology of preference – so I think that we can only take them to be appealing to some supposedly self-evident principle here. I should like to give this principle a grand title. 'The Principle of the Conservation of Evil across Chain Connections' would be appropriate, but that is a mouthful so I'll stick to 'principle A'. I take this principle to be the following.

Principle A: For any effect, E, of a cause, C, or of causes, $C-C^n$, E is evil only if C, or at least one member of $C-C^n$, is evil.

In other words, evil effects must have (at least some) evil causes. The logical contradiction in question arises because, on the strength of their endorsement of principle A, one would also expect libertarians to endorse the following: 'The Principle of the Conservation of *Good* across Chain Connections' or 'principle B'.

Principle B: For any effect, E, of a cause, C, or of causes, $C-C^n$, E is good only if C, or at least one member of $C-C^n$, is good.

One would expect this because 'evil' and 'good', being amongst the most general terms of evaluation we have, are members of the same category. One would therefore expect them to be symmetrical in the sense of sharing logical or grammatical features at the most general level. And indeed, this does seem to be the case, as the following fairly uncontroversial considerations illustrate. 'Good' and 'evil' are mutually exclusive in the sense that a thing cannot be both at the same time, at least (an important qualification) not in exactly the same respect. The claim that a thing, person or situation is good stands in need of justification in terms of reasons which appeal to certain of its features, and the same goes for the claim that a thing or situation is evil; reasons for thinking a thing is *morally* good are universalisable in the sense that they commit one to the claim that any other thing, similar in the relevant respects, is also good. Reasons for thinking a thing morally evil are also universalisable in this way. I leave it to the reader to extend the list.[2]

Now, if 'good' and 'evil' are symmetrical in this way, then it is possible to think of both principles as corollaries of an even more general principle, thus

The Principle of the Conservation of Moral Qualities Across Chain Connections: For any effect, E, of a cause, C, or of causes, $C-C^n$, E possesses moral quality, Q, only if C, or at least one member of $C-C^n$, possesses Q.

If this is right, then the two more specific principles, A and B, stand or fall together. Either both are true or neither is. The trouble is that libertarians are committed by the invisible hand thesis, to which I now turn, to the *denial* of the latter.

For an especially graphic example, consider Bernard Mandeville, who libertarians sometimes venerate for his famous *Fable of the Bees or Private Vices, Publick Benefits*. In just one verse of the poem which introduces the fable, *The Grumbling Hive or Knaves Turn'd Honest*, 'Avarice', 'Prodigality', 'Luxury', 'odious Pride', 'Envy', 'Vanity', 'Fickleness' and 'Inconstancy' are all said to contribute unwittingly to the general well-being. Avarice, prodigality and so on are fairly disreputable, and Mandeville *positively revels* in the contrast between the beneficent outcome and the turpitude of the motives from which it arises. That is the point of the poem. In other words, Mandeville is committed to the claim that good effects can sometimes arise from evil causes; that is, to the denial of principle B. In fact, at one point (quoted approvingly by Hayek)[3] Mandeville says this:

> the grand principle that makes us social creatures, the solid basis, the life and support of all trade and employment without exception is *evil*.
>
> (Mandeville 1970)

You couldn't put it plainer than that. The same consideration applies to Smith. Smith's butchers, brewers and bakers are, admittedly, more sober, more Presbyterian, and there is nothing so strikingly or positively evil about the self-interest from which they act. But then there is nothing too morally terrific about it either and, as Smith says, 'I have never known much good done by those who affected to trade for the public good' (1976, I: 478). So the point holds nevertheless. If it *were* true that good effects can only arise from good causes then it would have to be false that persons acting from 'regard to their own interest' are 'led by an invisible hand to promote the public good'. (In any case, I doubt that Smith would think his conclusion much affected by the consideration that brewers and bakers do sometimes act from positively evil motives.)

In conclusion, then, whereas the reducibility thesis presupposes the truth of principle A, the invisible hand thesis presupposes the falsity of principle B. But either both principles hold true or neither does. In effect, libertarianism is committed to claiming that the, more general, principle of the conservation of moral qualities is both true and false at the same time. This it cannot be. If I am right, this means that libertarianism is seriously broken backed in the sense that it must abandon one of its central theses.

My advice would be to abandon both and go in search of a more credible doctrine. Considerations of logical consistency apart, the falsity of the reducibility thesis can be fairly easily demonstrated with the help of a couple of simple counter-examples. First, take a chair – any chair. It is in one sense true enough of any chair that it is 'nothing more than' the sum of its discrete parts. For the sake of argument (and ignoring the exotically subatomic) let us assume these to be the individual molecules of which it is composed. If the same evaluative criteria applied to both whole and parts, as the thesis claims, then it would be impossible to evaluate a chair in the usual ways – as hard, green, ugly, uncomfortable, for example – because a molecule can be none of these things. The only alternative is to entertain the absurd possibility of there being hard, green, ugly and uncomfortable molecules.

For a second counter-example, this time with a temporal dimension added, consider: for reasons of personal hygiene, millions of individuals spray themselves with a small amount of underarm deodorant each morning. As a result, the ozone layer develops a hole, the globe warms up, polar ice-caps start to melt, and the demise of the human race starts to look a distinct possibility. Sir Keith Joseph thinks that an outcome can be evil only if the preferences which give rise to it are evil, so is he against personal hygiene or in favour of the demise of the human race? It's hard to believe that he is really either.

As for the invisible hand thesis, it may be true *sometimes* that evil preferences can give rise to good effects, but we have yet to find a good reason for thinking that this has to be the case, or even a reason for believing that it usually is.

2 MARKET ROMANCES

This is a good point at which to summarise the upshot of my discussion so far with a few comments of a more general nature, beginning with an observation on the resemblances between libertarianism and romantic love. The latter is sometimes said to be a sort of aspect-blindness. Somehow or other, the poor lover is rendered oblivious to even the most irritating mannerism, the crassest infidelity, the stalest odour. Likewise, libertarian theory in its more usual variants largely consists of strategies – reducibility, the freedom thesis, the invisible hand – which push capitalism's less attractive features beyond the perceptual field's margin, sometimes in the teeth of the evidence and, as we have just seen, in a way oblivious to contradictions. All too often the spell lifts too late, in the case of love with the midnight snore or, say, a creeping awareness of the crunching of toast. Or will the starry-eyed and oblivious continue to hold the faith, even in the face of what is now, as I write, routinely described as the worst recession since the 1930s?

This analogy with love also does something to illuminate an apparent paradox. Libertarianism isn't all bad, and there is, in particular, something very attractive indeed about the robust, no-nonsense emphasis some libertarian writers place on the importance of personal freedom. For example, Rothbard takes great pains to emphasise that 'Since sex is a uniquely private aspect of life, it is particularly intolerable that governments should presume to regulate and legislate sexual behaviour' (1973: 105) and comments with scorn on the public's 'irrational enthusiasm' for outlawing drugs (1973: 111). This is all well and good, but how is it that libertarianism's central tenets find the most favour with those most likely to disapprove of this sort of attitude; the narrowly moralistic advocates of repressive nuclear 'family values', the intolerant who treat all who step out of line (if they have no money) as parasites and wasters?[4] Is the explanation the usual one, the secret fascination of the monogamous bourgeois with the kinky? Or is it, in the words of Marx, just as in religion, 'the more man puts into God, the less he retains in himself' (1973: 108)? Maybe, but I doubt that either is the main explanation. I suspect that the truth is more mundane. It is just that libertarianism supplies the acquisitive and materialistic with a rationale for doing what they like doing best while adding the bonus that it enables them, at the same time, to feel moral about doing it.

Still, I know it is bad form to speculate on motives too much in a philosophical work, and, in any case, psychoanalysis is not my *forte*. From now on I shall try to ignore the causes of the infatuation and concentrate, as I have been for the most part, on showing that it is focused on an inappropriate object of desire. I realise that my words may do little to influence the infatuated. After all, infatuation is infatuation. I also have to consider that most of those sympathetic to libertarianism's tenets tend to be politically conservative and, as Roger Scruton says, 'argument is not the favourite pursuit of conservatives' (1980: 15). (Scruton is hardly conservativism's severest critic, so we can take him to be putting the point politely.) Conservatives who don't like to argue or think are unlikely to be impressed by arguments which, like the argument presented in the previous section of this chapter, appeal to logical relationships between very general principles. However, more thoughtful conservatives might care to reflect that libertarianism is about all the Right has in the way of a potentially credible theoretical justification for the ethical stances it tends to take. There is also the sort of traditionalism advanced by Burke, Oakeshott and Scruton himself – the traditionalism which supplies the non-thinking conservatives Scruton describes with a rationale and a moral justification for not bothering to think. So whether I am right depends on whether this amounts to a genuine, philosophically defensible theoretical position or whether it is just (as I suspect) a supercilious quasi-mysticism.[5] Still, that is another story.

Chapter 5

On freedom

I asserted earlier that Sir Isaiah Berlin's account of freedom is misleading and confused. In this chapter, I offer some arguments to support this claim. Here, then, is the famous passage from Berlin's 'Two Concepts of Liberty'; the one echoed by Joseph and Sumption, as by so many others.

> I am normally said to be free to the degree to which no man or body of men interferes with my activity. Political liberty in this sense is simply the area within which a man can act unobstructed by others. If I am prevented by others from doing what I could otherwise do, I am to that degree unfree; and if this area is contracted by other men beyond a certain minimum, I can be described as being coerced, or, it may be, enslaved. Coercion is not, however, a term that covers every form of inability. If I say that I am unable to jump more than ten feet in the air, or cannot understand the darker pages of Hegel, it would be eccentric to say that I am to that degree enslaved or coerced. Coercion implies the deliberate interference of other human beings within the area in which I could otherwise act. You lack political liberty only if you are prevented from attaining a goal by human beings. Mere incapacity to attain a goal is not lack of political freedom. This is brought out by the use of such modern expressions as 'economic freedom' and its counterpart, 'economic slavery'. It is argued, very plausibly, that if a man is too poor to afford something on which there is no legal ban – a loaf of bread, a journey round the world, recourse to the law courts – he is as little free to have it as he would be if it were forbidden him by law. If my poverty were a kind of disease, which prevented me from buying bread, or paying for the journey round the world or getting my case heard, as lameness prevents me from running, this inability would not naturally be described as a lack of freedom, least of all political freedom.

> (1969: 122–3)

I think the resemblance between this and the passage from Joseph and Sumption's book I quoted earlier will be apparent enough. I have also claimed that the sort of account of freedom outlined by Berlin has become an influential received orthodoxy, so to illustrate the point – and also to show that I am not singling Sumption and Sir Keith out for special opprobrium (just ordinary opprobrium) – let me give a few more examples. Note that all the writers quoted below take great pains to stress that it is, as they think, a confusion to equate the lack of freedom with the lack of ability or power. Each invites us to draw the conclusion that only the direct and so to speak face-to-face interference of one person with another can intelligibly be said to constitute a violation of liberty, and this – as I pointed out earlier – runs counter to my own view of the relation between capitalism and freedom. If they are right, then I am deeply misguided in holding that such violations can result from the routine and, as it were, 'blind' operation of market forces. Note also that the following quotations are all drawn from works written with the overt purpose of discrediting the Left.

F.A. Hayek – the first example – thus describes the confusion of freedom with power as having become 'dangerous' since it 'was deliberately fostered as part of the socialist argument', and he writes

> Neither of these confusions of individual liberty with different concepts denoted by the same word is as dangerous as its confusion with a third use of the word . . . the use of 'liberty' to describe the physical 'ability to do what I want', the power to satisfy our wishes, or the extent of the choice of alternatives open to us. This kind of 'freedom' appears in the dreams of many people in the form of the illusion that they can fly, that they are released from gravity and can move 'free like a bird' to wherever they wish, or that they have the power to alter their environment to their liking.[1]

> (1960: 16)

The following passage from Nozick's *Anarchy, State, and Utopia* is directed against the Marxian view that disadvantaged workers are coerced into accepting unpalatable wage offers.

> Some readers will object to my speaking frequently of voluntary exchanges on the grounds that some actions (for example, workers accepting a wage position) are not really voluntary because one party faces severely limited options, with all the others being much worse than the one he chooses. Whether a person's actions are voluntary depends on what it is that limits his alternatives. If facts of nature do so, the actions

are voluntary. (I may voluntarily walk to someplace I would prefer to fly to unaided.)

(1974: 262)

Antony Flew has the following to say on behalf of the (self-styled) National Association for Freedom, which, as British readers will know, is a very right-wing organisation. Like Berlin, Flew is keen to allege that freedom can only be violated by others deliberately.

The semantic crux with political freedom – the crux, that is, about the meaning of the expression 'political freedom' – makes no reference to what the agent is or is not either capable of doing or inclined to do, nor even to what is actually felt to be burdensome or confining. Freedom in this political understanding simply is the absence of coercion or constraint by other people: whether these human obstacles are such as make it physically impossible to follow some course; or whether they consist in sanctions applied to those who take it.[2]

(1978: 156)

Finally, Tibor R. Machan, who goes so ludicrously far as to equate Berlin's negative/positive freedom distinction with that between the 'libertarian, capitalist sort' of freedom (good) and the 'authoritarian or paternalist sort' ('collectivist' and bad) (1986: 50), writes as follows:

This concept of 'unfree' is a non-concept. I am not unfree to fly because I lack wings, nor am I unfree to study dodo birds because they no longer exist. One sometimes hears the term 'free' used this way but it is purely derivative.[3]

(1989: 217)

I could extend the list, but it is already long enough to make the point. Notice the extreme brevity with which my sort of view is dismissed. For example, Nozick's three sentence argument beginning 'Whether a person's actions are voluntary depends . . .' is all *Anarchy, State, and Utopia* has to offer in the way of a conceptual analysis of freedom, and yet Nozick feels able to erect his huge libertarian edifice on its foundation. In fact, the more recent the quotation, the briefer and more supercilious in tone it seems to be. Nozick must think it plain obvious that 'facts of nature' can never render an action non-voluntary, and the tone of Machan's remark implies that anyone holding my sort of view must be hopelessly simple minded, if not completely out to lunch.

Such certitude is the classic symptom of ossified dogmatism, and it is quite misplaced, as I shall try to show through an analysis of what Berlin has to say in the passage with which I opened. Perhaps I should warn the reader that this sort of exercise can become very 'picky' and analytical. However, I think I have succeeded in not straying too far from the main point within the body of this chapter, even where it isn't obvious that I have.[4]

1 DEFINING 'FREEDOM'

Readers familiar with 'Two Concepts of Liberty' will be well aware of just how open to interpretation it is. This isn't all bad. Such openness can often be the source of the capacity to inspire. Nevertheless, we ought to begin by trying to be clear about exactly what Berlin's view that freedom is essentially a 'negative' conception amounts to. I shall call this his 'negativism' for short.

1.1 The blocking model

For all I know, there may still be people around who hold the once popular but naive view that the job of a philosopher is to come up with definitions; definitions such as 'Truth is . . .'; 'Happiness is . . .'; 'Space and Time are . . .'; or, for the subject of this chapter, 'Freedom is . . .' After years of agonising thought and pages of argument, the rabbit is finally pulled from the hat in the form of the neat, three, four, five, six or so word phrase with which the blank can be filled in. Perhaps this is sometimes possible, but, in the case of freedom, I doubt very much that all there is to be said on the subject of such a complex concept can be summarised by a short formula. Even if it can, I shan't bother myself with the problem here, or play the game of trying to produce a definition of my own. All I shall try to do is develop an argument which rests upon what can, for sure, be said on the subject of freedom and leave it at that.

One noteworthy feature of the passage from 'Two Concepts' is that it shows that Berlin holds something like this naive and popular view. Of course, Berlin is not *that* naive. We are offered more than one line. We are offered a whole paragraph beginning, not with 'Freedom is . . .', but with 'I am normally said to be free when . . .'. However, we can take it that Berlin intends the paragraph to summarise the essentials of what he takes freedom to be. (He clearly believes there to be such things as 'essentials'.) Also, we are offered not so much a formula, but a model. The central idea motivating Berlin's account is, thus, that freedom is essentially a matter of there being a 'sphere' or 'area' within which the individual can act. The individual is said to be free to the extent to which he or she can move around within the area, unfree when prevented from moving beyond its confines. You are alleged to lack freedom only when your action is, so to speak, 'blocked'; so I shall call this model *the blocking model*.

The core of Berlin's view is that the concept of freedom, in all its manifold aspects, can be interpreted in the light of the blocking model; that, if you like, all there is to be said about freedom, or its lack, can be squeezed within the model's confines or stretched across its framework. This is the claim of which I am sceptical. It is not that I disagree with some of the remarks he makes. In fact it would be impossible to disagree with some of these; that I lack freedom, for example, 'if I am prevented by others from doing what I could otherwise do', if I am 'coerced' or if I am 'enslaved'. Berlin is also right to point out that my inability to jump ten feet in the air does not provide a reason for claiming that I am unfree to jump that high. However, the context in which these remarks occur makes it clear that Berlin thinks of himself as engaged in a boundary-marking exercise. Having postulated the blocking model, Berlin is presupposing that the remaining task is to specify what sorts of 'blocks' or obstacles count as genuinely freedom-restricting. It is as if he thinks it possible to eventually come up with a definition beginning, 'You lack freedom if, and *only* if . . .' and then proceed to fill in the blank with a long list of different types of obstacle.

It is the usefulness of this approach that I question. I realise that there are some simple and obvious cases which match the model exactly. For example, the prisoner in the exercise yard is clearly free to move within an area but unfree to move beyond it thanks to the high surrounding fence. However, the question is whether *all* cases of freedom or its restriction can be accurately described by analogy with this.

1.2 Blocking and negativism ('weak' and 'strong')

All proponents of negativism hold that we gain a greater understanding of the concept through an examination of the ways freedom can be limited or compromised – that is, by asking when it is that a person is *not* free – than we do from seeking out any chimerical 'positive' characteristics which free actions supposedly possess. Berlin's account, with its insistence that the presence or absence of preventing obstacles is the decisive factor (as opposed to the character of the action itself) is clearly, and as he says, 'negative' in this sense.

But within this definition of negativism, great variations are possible. For example, even within the confines of the 'analytic' or 'ordinary language' philosophy of the late 1950s and early 1960s the idea that the concept of freedom is essentially 'negative' in character did not originate with Berlin. One also finds it expressed in J.L. Austin's famous essay 'A Plea for Excuses' (1970). (Austin's essay was originally published in 1956, Berlin's 'Two Concepts' in 1958.) It is less often noticed than it ought to be that, despite a similarity of terminology, Berlin's and Austin's views are not at all equivalent. Let me outline the differences, taking Austin first. Austin writes:

> While it has been the tradition to present this ['freedom'] as the 'positive' term requiring elucidation, there is little doubt that to say we acted 'freely' (in the philosopher's use, which is only faintly related to the everyday use) is to say only that we acted *not* un-freely, in one or other of the many heterogeneous ways of so acting (under duress, or what not). Like 'real', 'free' is only used to rule out the suggestion of some or all of its recognised antitheses.
>
> (1970: 180)

According to Austin 'our common stock of words embodies all the distinctions men have found worth drawing, and the connections they have found worth marking, in the lifetimes of many generations', and the method he consequently recommends involves 'field work', the careful description and classification of these in order to 'dispose of the problem of Freedom' (1970: 183). This means that the whole thrust of Austin's argument runs in a direction quite contrary to that of Berlin's. For Austin, the distinctions embodied in 'our common stock of words' are diverse and manifold. They are 'likely to be more numerous, more sound . . . and more subtle, at least in all ordinary and reasonably practical matters, than any you or I are likely to think up in our arm-chairs of an afternoon' (1970: 182), all of which renders the likelihood of construing freedom on a single model extremely low. It also means that the Austinian negativist – the 'weak' negativist, as I shall call the proponent of this type of theory – has no need to speak in terms of 'spheres' or 'areas' at all. Where such terms are employed by this type of theorist, if they are, they need be no more than illustrative metaphors. We don't have to take them any more seriously than that. In contrast to Austin, as noted, Berlin stresses the notions of the area and the preventing obstacle a great deal. Are we to take this equally metaphorically? I think not, and for the purposes of my own argument I shall interpret Berlin as advancing a form of what I shall call 'strong' negativism. Before I say why, just to make sure that I've made the point clear, let me summarise what I take the distinction between 'weak' and 'strong' negativism to be.

First, weak (Austinian) negativism is, in effect, the claim that freedom is merely the absence of *constraint*. That might seem tautologously uninformative, 'constraint' being definable as 'anything which limits freedom', but for Austin it gains bite from the supposed existence of a constituency of ordinary language using antithesis recognisers capable of telling the genuine constraint from the bogus. The supposition may or may not be questionable, but – in any case – I have no particular quarrel to pick with it here. The main point is that – second, and by contrast – strong (Berlin style) negativism is the doctrine that freedom is the absence of obstacles *sufficient to prevent* action. The two doctrines are distinct because, although obstacles can be counted as constraints, 'constraint' is also wider than 'obstacle'. It includes more. For example, the fence surrounding the exercise yard is clearly an obstacle and, limiting the prisoner's freedom as it does, it is also a constraint. On the other hand, suppose that I have promised to visit my aunt tonight, so I now have a prior obligation, and that I cite this as a reason for being 'unable' to visit you. ('I am not free to come tonight', I say.) The obligation, or maybe my sense of obligation, is a constraint but it is *not* an obstacle. There is nothing actually – literally – preventing me from coming. I *could* come if I were prepared to break my promise. The distinction is important because it means that the strong negativist, unlike the 'weak', must take the blocking model, with its emphasis on the preventing obstacle *literally*.

1.3 Taking blocking seriously

I shall construe Berlin as a strong negativist throughout, but is this fair? Although I concede that interpreting him this way involves a certain amount of artifice I think it is, because, in my view, strong negativism is the view of freedom which is the most in line with what are evidently Berlin's central intentions.

For example, consider a piece of evidence drawn from amongst Berlin's more detailed remarks. Berlin insists that a person's *wants* are irrelevant to the determination of his or her freedom to act; that 'the definition of negative liberty as the ability to do what one wishes – which is, in effect, the definition adopted by Mill – will not do' because it would follow that 'If I find that I am able to do little or nothing of what I wish, I need only contract or extinguish my wishes, and I am made free' (1969: 139). On this view, the presence of a barrier across, say, Acacia Avenue, would render everyone in the world unfree to drive along it even if no one wanted to. This is fair enough (the prisoner is unfree to leave the exercise yard even if he or she has no wish to) *provided* that one treats the blocking model, according to which only obstacles count, as decisive. (Is a barrier across a street hundreds of miles away, along which one has no desire to travel, even a 'constraint'? A weak negativist might not wish to count it as such; although it is certainly an obstacle.)

But mainly, there is the fact that 'Two Concepts of Liberty' would lack its stated point unless we think of Berlin as a strong negativist. The whole point of the essay is to rule certain 'positive' interpretations of freedom out on the grounds that they are perversions of the idea that liberty 'consists in being one's own master'. Some examples given by Berlin are: the attempt to liberate oneself by extinguishing desires one knows one cannot realise; the identification of freedom with the control of desires one does not wish to have; the identification of liberation with the recognition of one's place within the realm of necessity; its identification with a legal system all rational persons can accept. There is no doubt that at least some of these interpretations do involve distortions of the concept; but the point is that the 'weak' negativist couldn't possibly rule them out as such, at least not all of them. For the latter, provided that there exist ordinary language users of whom it can legitimately be said that they treat some factor as a constraint on freedom, it must qualify as such. To take an example, Berlin writes of 'liberation through the extinction of desire' that 'This is the traditional self-emancipation of ascetics and quietists, of stoics or Buddhist sages' (1969: 135). If he is right, then such a group exists for this constraint, and weak negativism cannot disqualify it as Berlin would like. Only strong negativism, with its insistence on the literal interpretation of the blocking model can do so; and only strong negativism can do the job Berlin requires 'the notion of "negative" freedom' to do.

Put it this way: if this were an exercise in literary criticism it would probably be necessary to 'place' Berlin's text in all its aspects, to do detailed justice to its many nuances and ambiguities, and so on. But this is philosophy, and the aim is to get to the truth about freedom.

2 THE GANGSTER, THE HYPNOTIST, THE PIT

Berlin, like Austin, frequently appeals to 'common sense' facts of ordinary usage. This tends to obscure the difference between the two philosophers, and to disguise the fact that, for each, the function of such appeals is quite different. In Berlin's case, their main function is supposed to be to reinforce a particular presupposition - that the blocking model is adequate. In fact, as I shall now go on to argue, they do not. Some sit uneasily with Berlin's central claim, and others are inconsistent with it. As I shall point out, taking blocking seriously means that some of the factors Berlin wants to count as freedom-restricting cannot be counted as such. It also means that some of the factors he does not want to count at all have to be included.

2.1 Blocking and coercion

For a start, taking blocking seriously means that Berlin cannot even count *coercion* as a violation of liberty. This is disastrous for Berlin's position, because if anything is absolutely uncontroversial in this area it is that coercion and liberty stand opposed. Coercion is – in Austin's phrase – one of freedom's 'recognised antitheses'.

But now consider the following standard, 'textbook' example of coercion: A person, A, is waylaid by a gangster who threatens A with a gun: 'Your money or your life'. A prefers staying alive to keeping the money, so A hands the money over. A clearly lacks freedom in this example, and – indeed – we have at our disposal a number of stock expressions with which to articulate the fact. For example, when A hands the money over, A does not perform a 'free action'; A does not act out of his or her 'own free will' or 'voluntarily'; A's action is 'not fully his or her own'; A is 'subject to the will of another', and so on.

A would prefer to keep the money and stay alive, but this option is ruled out by the gangster's threat. Let us now ask: is there, in this example, an obstacle sufficient to prevent A both keeping the money and staying alive? If there is, the example may match the blocking model. If there is not, it doesn't. The answer to the question is *not necessarily* because, for all I have said so far, it could be that the gangster's gun is only a toy, a plastic replica recently purchased from Woolworth's. In this case, there will be no obstacle in A's way; the gangster couldn't possibly shoot A dead, and it will be open to A to walk away from the situation as he or she likes.

The point is this: where A fails to realise the true nature of the situation it will, nevertheless, remain the case that A is coerced. It follows that blocking negativism, according to which a person lacks freedom if, and only if, he or she is confronted by a preventing obstacle, is false. Let me stress this conclusion: it cannot be the case *both* that coercion violates freedom *and* that the concept of freedom is essentially negative in the sense of 'negative' Berlin's argument requires. And further, since it is true that coercion violates freedom, Berlin's account of the concept must be false.

2.2 Negative freedom and positive freedom

The foregoing conclusion is not surprising in a way. All the example does is illustrate the fact that, in standard cases of coercion, the operative factor is the victim's *belief* that some or other undesirable consequence will follow unless he or she complies with the threat. The actual presence or absence of an obstacle is therefore irrelevant to the classification of the case as a case of coercion. In the example, A hands the money over because A believes the gangster will shoot. The belief is false, but the point would apply equally if the gangster's gun were real. If A thought the threat empty, A wouldn't comply. (A might end up being shot, but A's defiant or foolhardy action would be free enough.) Cases of coercion are, therefore, different from those cases which clearly and uncontroversially match the blocking model; and where the restriction of liberty results from what is self-evidently an obstacle, what Berlin says of wants goes for beliefs too. For example, the prisoner is prevented from escaping by the fence whatever he believes about its presence. If he tries to ignore it – to walk through it, for example – it will stop him just the same.

Nor can I see how the proponent of negativism could possibly avoid the conclusion without relaxing the blocking model. For example, I think it likely that many readers will want to respond to the argument surrounding the 'gangster' case by insisting that, although it is true that there is, strictly speaking, no obstacle facing A, there is nevertheless a *sense* of 'obstacle' in which other factors, such as A's belief *can* be counted as obstacles. However, the problem with this response is that it invokes the same sense of 'obstacle' as my obligation to visit my aunt is an obstacle to my visiting you; whereas the 'strictly speaking' is all important here. *Genuine* obstacles – obstacles 'strictly speaking', walls and fences – prevent *absolutely*, whether or not anyone believes they are present. Other obstacles are only obstacles by analogy. This means that the only way to avoid the conclusion is to shift from a 'strong' to a 'weak' negativist position. As we have noted, if Berlin were to do this the talk of spheres and areas would become redundant, and his argument would be deprived of its central point.[5]

In conclusion, it seems to me that philosophers who continue to insist that freedom is, in some way, 'essentially' negative ought to ask themselves what the *point* of this insistence is. Either they are making the patently false claim that only 'strictly speaking' obstacles count as genuine restrictions of freedom, or else they are claiming that it is somehow useful or illuminating to try to assimilate all constraints within a metaphor of spheres and areas. Now, I realise that this latter move is, in a way, in line with ordinary usage, but there are ways in which ordinary usage can obscure real differences between cases. Philosophy ought to help remove the obscurity, not incorporate it within a theory. For example, in colloquial speech it is quite usual and unobjectionable to describe laws as barriers, to say of some person that he or she was unable to do such-and-such because of the existence of some law, and so on. But in the usual case – where you refrain from parking on a yellow line, say – that is not, in fact, usually because there is some obstacle in your way, something you would crash against, or, maybe, some pit you would fall into were you to try. (If there were, you wouldn't have to refrain.) You *can* park on the line and in that sense (the sense captured by the blocking model) you are perfectly free to. What stops you – what makes you refrain – is not an obstacle but the fear, the knowledge of what might happen if you were to be caught.

In my view, there is no point in trying to classify coercion artificially with more obvious cases of blocking, and I suggest that we gain more insight if we group it, instead, with other cases of manipulation, cases in which one person 'subjects another to his or her will'. After all, that is what the gangster tries to do. If he could, he might attach ropes to *A*'s limbs and move *A* this way and that like a puppet, or he might hypnotise *A*. He can't do either of these things, but he can threaten *A*. In the case of hypnotism, note, although *A* is clearly not a free agent there are quite evidently *no* obstacles confronting *A*.

If we look at it this way, we also get another interesting result for it means we have to think of the victim of coercion as lacking the freedom Berlin describes in the following terms.

> I wish my life and decisions to depend on myself, not on external forces of whatever kind. I wish to be an instrument of my own, not of other men's, acts of will. I wish to be a subject, not an object; to be moved by reasons, by conscious purposes, which are my own, not by causes which affect me, as it were, from outside. I wish to be somebody, not nobody; a doer – deciding, not being decided for, self-directed and not acted upon by external nature or by other men as if I were a thing, or an animal, or a slave incapable of playing a human role, that is, of conceiving goals and policies of my own and realising them.
>
> (1969: 131)

In short, we have to view coercion as a violation of what Berlin calls *positive* freedom.

2.3 Blocking and deliberate interference

Just as the blocking model, consistently interpreted, must exclude coercion, so it must include obstacles or barriers which have not been deliberately placed in an agent's way by other persons and count them as restrictions of freedom. As the passage under discussion makes clear, Berlin is very concerned to deny this; to stress that you lack freedom 'only if you are prevented from attaining a goal by other human beings'. However, the blocking model can make no relevant distinction between the causes of obstacles, personal or impersonal. It entails that the boulder blocking your path renders you unfree to continue your journey, whether it has been put there by the police or whether its presence results, not from personal agency, but from an avalanche. (Berlin may be right to point out, as he does, that *coercion* 'implies the deliberate interference of other human beings' but, as we have seen, coercion is a different story.)

Berlin appeals to a number of simple 'common sense' examples to support his 'deliberate interference only' claim ('If I say that I am unable to jump more than ten feet . . .' and so on) so let us note that a similar appeal can be used to suggest that his claim has an absurd implication. Thus: suppose that you are kidnapped and thrown into a deep (naturally formed) pit from which you cannot escape. Suppose that, later, an unfortunate passer-by just happens to fall into the pit with you, by accident. If Berlin were right, you would be unfree to leave the pit, because someone has deliberately put you there, whereas the passer-by, whose predicament results from gravitational force alone, would be free to leave at any time but simply incapable of so doing. This seems an odd conclusion to draw, if only because you are both caught in the same trap. Nor, to continue the story a little, can it be right to say that the death or departure of the only person who can release you liberates you both – even though you remain in the pit – as the 'deliberate interference only' principle would appear to imply on the grounds that your plight is no longer dependent on human agency. (By the way, this is the appropriate place to point out that Berlin's occasional qualification of 'liberty' with the adjective 'political' can be safely ignored. However, I confine the explanation of why to a note.)[6]

3 DELIBERATE INTERFERENCE, FACTS OF NATURE, MARKET FORCES

Just to summarise: if one construes the claim that freedom is essentially negative in a way that would permit Berlin to draw his central conclusion – i.e. that 'positive' accounts of freedom are misguided – one is forced, first, to deny that coercion violates liberty and, second, to count factors which do not result from deliberate human agency as freedom-restricting. Berlin would welcome neither implication. ('Weak' negativists are not so forced, but then they also define 'positive' freedom differently.) Nor would libertarians, who want to deny that the routine operation of market forces limits liberty. They must also construe negativism in the way Berlin does and the same consequences are thus logically forced upon them. Let us now examine this point more closely.

3.1 Negativism and libertarianism

So far as libertarianism is concerned, the main conclusion to be drawn from my argument so far is that the neat, homiletic little passages with which libertarians seek to support their freedom thesis – the genuflections to authority and 'sense' (Flew's, Nozick's, Machan's) – in fact settle nothing. Exert a little pressure in the right places, and they fall apart before one's eyes.

Now, it is difficult to tell for sure, but I don't think it would be reading too much into such passages to say that there appears to be an argument underlying them; one which surrounds the following four claims;

Claim 1 Freedom is essentially negative in the sense that all genuine cases of freedom and its restriction match the blocking model.

Claim 2 A person's freedom can only be limited by the deliberate interference of another person.

Claim 3 It is a misuse of language to describe an inability which results from the routine operation of an all-pervading natural force, such as gravity, as a lack of freedom.

Claim 4 Likewise, it is a misuse of language to describe an inability resulting from the routine operation of a market force as a lack of freedom.

The suggestion seems to be that, since claim 1 is true, the truth of claim 2 follows; that this, in turn, entails the truth of claim 3 and consequently that of claim 4. Against this, as I have argued, claim 1 is false; but even if it were true it would entail the *falsity* of claims 2, 3 and 4, not their truth. For libertarians, and just as one might expect, the real point is to establish claim 4. If claim 4 were true, then it really would be the case that the market is a unique respecter of freedom, and the suggestion is that a negativism along the lines of that advanced by Berlin entails that claim's truth. However, it should be clear by now that, following the most consistent interpretation to which it is open, Berlin's negativism does nothing of the kind. (To put it in terms of Berlin's own example, it entails, contra Berlin himself, that the person too poor to afford bread really is unfree to buy bread.)

That said, though, might there not be other reasons for drawing the libertarian conclusion, reasons which are independent of Berlin's 'official' negativist stance? There might be, because there do, on the face of it, seem to be two independent reasons for accepting claim 3. Berlin offers one in the form of his 'common sense' appeals to a certain type of simple example

– the type of example in which a person is obviously *free* to do some given action, but is nevertheless *unable* to do it. This seems right. If you are standing at the shallow end of a swimming pool, and there is nothing or no one blocking your way, and so on, then you are free to swim a length. The fact that you are completely unable to swim would seem to have absolutely no bearing on this freedom. As Berlin puts it, 'If I say that I am unable to jump more than ten feet in the air . . . it would be eccentric to say that I am to that degree enslaved or coerced' (1969) and – as I would add – not just 'enslaved' or 'coerced' but unfree in any relevant respect (and the same goes for Sir Keith Joseph on Latin hexameters).

In addition to this, there is the point – a point which seems to me to lend a certain unspoken force to Berlin's argument – that there really is something deeply misguided, absurd even, in treating every natural limitation as a restriction of freedom. For example, Nozick is right to insist that 'I may voluntarily walk to someplace I would prefer to fly to unaided' *if* this is interpreted to mean that Nozick is nonetheless a *free agent* even though he can't fly. The routine and usual effects of a natural force – the gravity which holds you to the ground when you walk to the supermarket, say – do not obstruct action but, rather, they define the parameters within which free action becomes possible. Treating such phenomena as obstructions to freedom would also carry the absurd implication that only some superbeing, capable of independent flight, instantaneous movement across vast distances, and even more incredible feats, could be counted as a 'truly free' agent. This implication would not do justice to the distinction which is really at issue when we separate the free from the unfree. In any self-respecting treatise on determinism such points will be regarded as truistic, and Berlin's essay echoes this.

Let us now consider these points in turn, taking Berlin's 'jumping' example first.

3.2 Why can't I jump ten feet?

So, innocuous though it may appear, Berlin's 'jumping' example is clearly worth unpicking, if only because examples like it are so often required to bear so much theoretical weight. I agree with Berlin that it would be 'eccentric' to describe someone as being unfree to jump ten feet just because he or she is unable to, but the first point to stress is that Berlin, like the libertarian, needs more than this. The 'eccentricity' has to be shown to entail *the generalisation* (claim 3) that the routine operation of a natural force can *never* be said to limit liberty. I do not believe it can. In my view, the apparent force of Berlin's argument derives only from the vagueness of his phrase, 'it would be eccentric to say that . . .'. As I shall argue in this section, this is broad enough to confuse *truth conditions* with *explaining factors.*

Let us ask: where exactly does the eccentricity lie? Note that Berlin's appeal to the 'jumping' example hinges on the distinction between – as I would put it – the *obstacle* and the *incapacity.* If obstacles and incapacities can be confused, that is presumably because either type of factor can function as the sufficient condition in an explanation of a person's inability to do some given action. That is, either an 'obstacle term' or an 'incapacity term' can substitute for *y* in an explanation of the form, '*A* was unable to do *x* because of *y*'. Nevertheless, obstacles and incapacities are different, and the difference lies in the relationship of each to the agent.

An obstacle, it seems reasonable to assume, is a feature of a person's environment. Moreover, it seems pretty clear that, to count as a preventing obstacle, a thing must be an *extra* feature of that environment, something which, as it were, blocks a space which would otherwise be available for an action to fill. This means, in turn, that to count a given factor as an obstacle one must have a conception of what it would be for a given agent to carry out the action at present obstructed. One knows what it would be for the prisoner to walk away from the exercise yard – one can picture the walking away – and one can consequently count the surrounding fence as the obstacle to that action. (It is at times like this that philosophy can seem a banal exercise in stating the obvious; and so it would be if the obvious weren't overlooked by so many 'significant' philosophical theses.)

In common with the 'blocking' negativist, I hold that, *if* there exists an obstacle sufficient to prevent person *A*'s doing action *x*, the fact is in turn sufficient to establish the truth of '*A* is unfree to do *x*'. Perhaps I should stress this. My quarrel with blocking negativism is not the truth of this claim. What I question is the truth of the claim that *all* cases of the restriction of freedom match the blocking model, so that *A* is unfree if, *and only if,* there is a preventing obstacle present. Bearing this in mind, *and supposing Berlin to be standing in the open,* it is equally evident that Berlin is, as he says, free to jump, not just ten feet but ten miles into the air. For a start, it is easy enough to picture him doing so (although he can't). All he would have to do (if he could) would be to bend his knees a little, push with his feet, and up he would go (and, in any case, we have all seen *Superman*). If there are no birds or low flying aircraft to block his route – if, in short, there are no obstacles – then Berlin is free to jump ten miles. But where is the eccentricity? In this case it would not be so much 'eccentric' as *plain false* to claim that Berlin lacks the freedom to jump.

The case will be different, though, if we suppose Berlin to be standing in a room with a ceiling less than ten feet (say nine feet) from the floor. There will now be an obstacle sufficient to prevent him jumping ten feet, and it will not only be not at all eccentric but it will be *true* to say that he lacks the freedom to jump ten feet. And since facts of nature are an issue here, note that it makes no difference if we suppose Berlin to be standing in a naturally formed, nine-foot high, cave. So far, then, we have no reason for accepting claim 3.

However – and here is the point – the truth or falsity of 'Berlin is free to jump ten feet' is one thing, whereas the *explanation* for his inability to jump ten feet is another. It is true enough that, were Berlin to attempt the feat while indoors, the ceiling would stop him even if nothing else did, but in fact the ceiling falls out of account, because Berlin, like most of us, couldn't jump nine feet if he tried, indoors or outdoors. Most of us are insufficiently athletic. Our bodies just aren't constructed that way. In short, we lack the *capacity* to jump, and the presence of any obstacles there may be is irrelevant to the explanation of our inability. Note that these features, insufficient athleticism and so on, cannot be counted as obstacles because they are not located in our surrounding environment but elsewhere. (In this case they are features of our bodies and therefore, in a fairly clear sense, of ourselves.)[7] This means that, although it would indeed be 'eccentric', because wrong, to *explain* the inability to jump ten feet in terms of a lack of freedom, it doesn't follow that it must be *false* that one lacks the freedom to jump ten feet, or that any inability resulting from a naturally placed obstacle cannot, without distortion, be described as a lack of freedom. Therefore, the 'jumping' example cannot be used to support claim 3, as libertarians would like.

3.3 'Facts of nature': market forces

So, what of the anti-determinist truism, the one Nozick invokes when he points out that he is quite free to achieve his destination, even though he has to walk there and cannot fly? It may be absurd to describe the routine effects of a very general fact of nature, such as gravity, as freedom restricting, but it is worth asking exactly why this should be. The obstacle/incapacity distinction suggests the following possible explanation. The effects of a force such as gravity are so all-pervasive and so uniform that we tend to treat them as inescapable features of the human condition, as part of the background within which we all move rather than as *extra* features of the environment which block actions we could otherwise do. We therefore tend to treat our inability to jump to great heights as an incapacity rather than as a lack of freedom. (Not that we should think of the obstacle/incapacity boundary as especially fixed. It is interesting to speculate on how things might change were travel to planets with weaker gravitational fields than our own to become commonplace. Libertarians who attach significance to the fact that the market is in some sense 'natural' might care to reflect on the implications of this possibility for their position.)

But this doesn't help, once again because libertarian arguments which rest on claim 3 require us to move from its being *sometimes* or even *usually* absurd to describe a natural limitation as a restriction on freedom to the general conclusion that it must *always* be so. The inference is invalid and its conclusion can, in any case, easily be shown to be false because, whatever the 'human condition' may be, it is undeniable that natural forces can sometimes place obstacles in one's way just as other people can. Thus, while the gravity which enables Nozick to walk may not compromise his liberty, it doesn't follow that the boulder and the fallen tree which block his path – and which have been set in place by the same gravity – are not obstacles which render him unfree to continue his journey.

The conclusion to be drawn at this point is as follows: if it were true that the effects of an all-pervading natural force in its routine operation cannot be said to restrict freedom (claim 3), then *with the assumption that a market force strictly resembles a natural force* (i.e. that it is similarly inescapable and ineluctable) it would follow that it is equally absurd to describe the effects of a market force, in its routine operation, as freedom-restricting (claim 4). However, it follows from the arguments I have presented here that claim 3 is false. This means that claim 4 cannot be derived from it.

Now, there are two reasons why it is more than a little surprising to find myself arguing for this conclusion. The first is that it is fairly apparent that there is no such strict resemblance between a natural force and a market force. As we have noted, the latter is the outcome of numerous bilateral market exchanges between market agents. Also, the framework within which those agents operate has to be held in place by, and can be altered by, laws defining rights of ownership and control. There are thus at least two respects in which a market force is the outcome of deliberate human agency. By contrast, gravity is 'just there'; so much a part of the background against which the drama of human life is played out that one would have to be rocketed deep into outer space to avoid it.

The second reason is that libertarians know this very well. It is true enough that two of libertarianism's most notable philosophers try to establish, each in his own way, that the market is somehow 'natural'; but neither tries to do so in the same sense that gravity is a 'natural' force. For example, Nozick thinks that we are born with 'natural' rights – rights which we naturally 'have' in much the way we naturally have kidneys, digestive tracts, and other bodily organs. The naturalness of the 'pure' free market thus flows – for Nozick – from the fact that it operates in a way which respects those rights. For Hayek, the market has grown over time. It is a 'spontaneous order' which has 'naturally' evolved in a manner similar to, but not precisely the same as, that in which biological organisms have evolved.[8] But neither Nozick nor Hayek would deny that force is sometimes needed to protect the rights-framework which enables the market to operate. After all, each is arguing that the framework should be set up one way rather than another. This makes it very unlikely that an argument which appeals to the relation between humans and gravity – to the fact that one is unable to jump ten feet in the air or fly to the supermarket and nevertheless one remains free – can have any relevance to the conclusions they wish to draw. (Even if claim 3 *were* true, it isn't obvious that claim 4 would follow.) And yet, as we have seen, both Nozick and Hayek, in common with many other libertarians, do sometimes tend to rely upon just such an argument.

4 CONCLUSIONS

The first conclusion to be drawn here is – clearly – that libertarianism can derive no logical support whatsoever from appeals to Berlin's 'Two Concepts of Liberty' or to the distinction he claims to detect between 'negative' and 'positive' notions of freedom.

The second is that there is, indeed, a real distinction to be drawn along something like Berlin's lines, but that the way the negative freedom/positive freedom story is usually told theoretically misconstrues the real distinction in a number of ways. Specifically, it tends to obscure the differences between the two ways in which a person can be rendered unfree. Thus, when it is asked of some person if he or she is free, the question is sometimes whether he or she is free from some obstruction to perform some action. It is 'What, if anything, blocks the action?' To find the answer we must go in search of an obstacle. But at other times, the question is 'Whose action is it?' For example, when A is robbed by the gangster, A is conforming, not to his or her own plans, but to the gangster's plans. In this case, that is what renders A 'subject to the will of another'.

What this means is that there is more than one model structuring the concept of freedom; not just the blocking model but, as I shall call it, 'the ownership model'.[9] Metaphorical or otherwise, repeated insistence on talk of 'areas' with their surrounding 'constraints' obscures this and prevents us from asking the right questions. For example, it prevents us from

attempting to determine precisely what criteria have to be satisfied before
it can be correctly said of someone that he or she is not, or not the 'full',
owner or 'author' of some action. Coercion by threats may not be the only
sort of case, of course. When Kate Millett writes of 'sexual politics' that it
'obtains consent through the "socialisation" of both sexes to basic patriar-
chal policies with regard to temperament, role, and status' (1972: 26), isn't
it at least plausible to say that the phenomenon she describes is – whatever
else it may be – something which compromises women's freedom? Some
might think not (see, for example, Sher 1983), but negativist tunnel vision
can prevent us from even beginning to look for an answer.

What is needed is a systematic philosophical account of the distinction
between 'fully' and 'only partly' owned actions – although I do not propose
to offer such an account here, only to point out that it is needed. Proponents of negativism are likely to protest against this that it must be
impossible to provide such an account without succumbing to 'totalitarian'
traps.[10] However, that cannot be right. It cannot be right because the
distinction is evidently there to be drawn, so the possibility of drawing it
while avoiding the traps exists. I do think it clear, though, that, wherever
the distinction lies, libertarian attempts to draw it in terms which rely on
the negativist metaphor of areas – of rights, 'boundaries' and so on – must
turn out to be hopelessly inadequate.

My third conclusion concerns the value of freedom. There is no point
in trying to demonstrate that some system such as the free market uniquely
respects freedom unless one can explain why freedom is important.
Otherwise, why should anyone care? For example, imagine a city, somewhere thousands of miles from where you live, somewhere you are never
likely to visit and do not even have the remotest interest in visiting. Now
suppose that roadworks are in progress and that the authorities have
placed a barrier across one of the city's main streets. City authorities being
what they are, your supposition will almost certainly be correct, and it will
also be true – as Berlin says – that you are now unfree to drive along that
street. But why should you care? You have no reason to care. Your lack
of a 'negative' freedom such as this can have no significance for you until
it starts to come into contact with your own wants, your preferences and
your plans (or maybe with your values – you may have a reason to object
if you take a general moral view on interference with the traffic flow). This
explains why we have to take the ownership model of freedom seriously.
More generally, it seems to me that a full account of freedom must connect
the value of freedom with the fact that humans are purposive creatures –
that they formulate goals and plans of their own in the hope of achieving
them – so much so that it is difficult to imagine a being that is not purposive

in this sense but which can be unproblematically classified as a person (hence many of the philosophical difficulties surrounding the moral status of the fetus, or the incurably 'brain dead', for example).[11] That is what self-styled and so-called libertarianism attempts to do; but it is unlikely to turn out that freedom as the full ownership of one's actions has much to do with an economic system which rests on the private ownership of possessions.

Chapter 6

The legend of the angels and the fable of the bees

The ancient legend runs as follows:

> Once – so long ago that it has almost been forgotten – people had wings.
> They were able to fly from place to place at will, like birds or angels.
> But then the gods became jealous and, feeling themselves threatened by
> this human ability to fly, they decided to remove it. This they did by
> binding up the people's wings, forcing them to travel only by foot.
> Generations passed, and people's wings became etiolated through lack
> of use until eventually they fell away like withered leaves. There was a
> time when, in moments of despair, people would go into the open and
> flex their shoulders uselessly; a sad and tragic ceremony. But even this
> is now long past. Few are aware that people once had wings, and, to all,
> the idea that we may one day fly like angels now appears a crazy illusion.

The legend isn't really so ancient, of course. In line with Wittgenstein's
advice that imaginary stories can sometimes be just as helpful as real ones
when it comes to getting a navigational fix on a concept, I've just made it
up. Or at least I think I have. The fact that so many philosophers of a
certain persuasion seem obsessed by the freedom (or 'freedom') to fly
makes me less sure. Perhaps there is, after all, some truth in the version of
the legend according to which, because the memory of flight persisted (as
it still does sometimes 'in the dreams of many people'), high priests of the
new order were appointed by the gods to reconcile the people to their
fallen state. 'I may voluntarily walk to someplace I would prefer to fly to
unaided'.[1] You too – so count yourself lucky you can walk! Their strategy,
in the manner characteristic of high priests, was to replace the old myth
with a new one; and according to this new myth we are not fallen,
earthbound angels at all, but potential bees.

What are we to make of these stories? Each portrays the human
condition in a way which captures a certain truth. For example, it is

beyond question that humans, like bees, are social creatures. For each species, the individual's conditions of existence – life itself usually – are dependent on the co-ordinated labours of the others. But the fable only highlights this truth by exaggerating it and thereby obscuring significant differences.

There is, for example, the fact that everything is done for the bee by evolution; so much so that it is possible to think of the individual bee as a mere component of the greater organism, the hive. Each part, each bee, moves automatically in a way which contributes to the survival and flourishing of the whole. If you want an example of a totalitarian system at work, there you have it *par excellence*. By contrast, for humans there is no such evolutionarily-placed guiding hand. We may be social creatures, but we are nevertheless imperfectly socialised and have only our wits to rely on. There is a connection between this difference and other great differences between humans and bees. A human is a self-conscious creature with a sense of identity; that is, the human is capable of envisioning the line demarcating his or her 'person' from the person of another. Within this line, the human formulates his or her 'own' beliefs, goals and plans. The human is a purposive creature, capable of acting on those plans. That's how we do it. We have to because, for us, there is *no guarantee* that all plans will magically harmonise for the sake of some greater good. None of this is true of the bee. The bee has no sense of identity and does not think. It does not have wits. The bee is a sort of natural machine. It does not act. It simply moves.

Still, I suppose it is hardly news that the Fable of the Bees isn't strictly or literally true, and perhaps we do it an injustice by treating it that way. After all, it was only ever meant to be a story and perhaps we should think of the truth it contains as the sort of literary or artistic truth, appropriate to stories. Perhaps; but if we do we should also bear in mind that the function of a story can vary according to the context in which it is told, and that something can also hang on who is telling it. We should remember, for example, the 'magnificent myth' or 'noble lie' which Plato put in the mouths of his philosopher rulers to help them establish control – 'one of those convenient stories' as he describes it in *The Republic* (1987: 181). As Plato says, it isn't literally true that people are born with base metals, iron or bronze, in their souls, but the idea is that if you can get them to believe this they will be reconciled to having missed out on privilege and higher education. Given the context, Plato's myth of the metals is more than innocent bedtime reading.

Something similar goes for the Fable of the Bees; it has a role to play within the context of a certain political vision. This makes it interesting to consider what one might find oneself saying if one were to try to persuade people that they are really bees.[2] It is, for example, interesting to see just how compatible the interpretation of freedom discussed in the previous chapter and the vision are. Thus, for the bee, it really is true that freedom is nothing more than, or 'simply', the absence of obstructions. That's because bees only move, so that the freedom of the bee is much like the freedom of the inanimate object – the metal ball which is 'free' to continue its roll down the inclined plane provided that nothing prevents it. You liberate the bee by opening the window, by removing the block which has been stopping it getting to the flower towards which it is instinctively propelled. A view of the world which accords humans and bees equivalent status is likely to portray the concept of human freedom as, likewise, exhausted by talk of blocks and their removal. Of course, the bee only ever 'wants' to do that which it has the capacity to do; that is, precisely what it will do provided there is nothing to prevent it. Unlike the human – or, which may come to the same thing, the fallen angel being transformed into a bee-person – it will never concern itself with other possibilities, with unrealisable ambitions or unattainable goals. The human will and, experiencing regret at these unrealised possibilities, will sometimes wish to imbue them with the qualities of present constraints. To this person, the teller of the fable can say: 'Don't worry. You have misunderstood and your regrets are of no consequence. Remember that no one can jump more than ten feet, and that, in any case, you are an aspiring bee.'

The 'negativist' account of freedom may not have a *logical* connection with the libertarian vision, but it seems that there is nevertheless a way in which it evidently helps. In a similar manner, the 'humans-as-bees' story will only legitimate wants appropriate to the latter. Bees are neither saints nor ascetics, they envision no other worlds, and, because the 'wants' of all bees are co-ordinated by evolution, the bee will only ever want to act for the greater good of the social whole. For fallen angels turning into bees, this means that the moment of liberation will finally arrive in the form of a massive attack of amnesia, when the bee-people finally forget for good that they were ever angels, and cease to feel that it is even worth trying to regain their wings. Friedman writes:

> Indeed, a major source of objection to a free economy is precisely that it does this task so well. It gives people what they want instead of what a particular group thinks they ought to want.

> (1962: 15)

So it will, once the bee people have forgotten what they once wanted. Or put it this way: 'The free economy gives you what you want if you want to be a bee. If you don't want to be a bee, it won't give you what you want. But bear in mind what you *ought* to want. You ought to want to be a bee.' Here, as so often with this type of writer, Friedman is guilty of a failing he is so ready to sarcastically deprecate in others. In this case, telling people what they ought to want, as in the previous quote.

I offer the Legend of the Angels as an antidote. Make of it what you will. Believe it if you like. For myself, I don't believe that humans are fallen angels, although I do think that we are a lot more like angels than we are often given credit for. Like the angels and unlike the bees we are capable of envisioning alternative possibilities. For us, it is conceivable that the world we inhabit might have been different from the way it actually is. We can also extend this criterion to ourselves. Might not we have been quite different? Might not we even have been able to fly? Maybe not, but that doesn't prevent us wanting to or striving at least some distance in the direction of the impossible.

Notice how things which look neat and simple when viewed from one perspective start to look less so when approached from another. For example, it seems right to say that you are, as Berlin says of jumping, free to fly but simply incapable of doing so. You may stand in the open, thus ensuring that there are no obstacles blocking your path, but however hard and for however long you move your shoulder blades this way and that you will never take off. But now suppose that the legend is true. If it is, you have a distant ancestor of whom it could rightly be said that he or she had the capacity to fly, but who was rendered unfree to fly by the deliberate interference of others. That, after all, is what the gods did when they bound up our wings. They took away one of our *freedoms*. Now ask, at what point in the story does it cease to be true of people that they are 'capable of flight but unfree to fly' and become true instead that they are 'free to fly but simply incapable of doing so'? For example, is it the point at which the first generation, the ones upon whom the dreadful deed was directly inflicted, have just died off, leaving their pedestrianised offspring – wings still intact but useless – to cope as best they can? The resemblance between parents and offspring is fairly close here, so it seems too early. To locate the temporal point here would be arbitrary in any case. So does it come several generations later, when wings are finally shed from human bodies? There seems to be no better reason for selecting this. Indeed, there seems to be no good reason for selecting *any* precise point on the line as conceptually crucial.

So, should we conclude from this that we are, after all, capable of flight at will? I don't think so, not us, not the human individuals who happen to be alive now. Moreover, the fact that a line is difficult to draw with precision does not mean that it isn't there to be crossed. The legend does nothing to call into question the accuracy of the descriptions at issue: 'able to but unfree to'; 'free to but unable to'. Rather, it questions the fixity of the categories they deploy and, as a consequence, their force; and it does this with a story which highlights the connection of generations.

I offer these remarks tentatively. To be honest, I am quite unsure exactly what to make of the legend myself, so I'll just add the following. The legend suggests a context in which a lack of capacity can also count as a lack of freedom. It suggests that it can count as such when it was once possessed by someone else to whom one is related in a certain way, for example – as in the legend – an ancestor. This suggests, in turn, that examples like Berlin's 'jumping' case miss something by concentrating too narrowly on specific individuals in specific situations at specific points in time; the person standing in the field and trying to jump, for example. Further, the legend suggests that there might be other relationships which also permit certain incapacities to be counted as unfreedoms. For example, it suggests how the paraplegic's present incapacity can count as a lack of a freedom to walk thanks to the relevant contrast between this and the capacities of his or her more able-bodied fellows. And what of future people; of our descendants, say? Might not a continuation of the story go as follows: remembering that we could once fly – and resisting the amnesia of the bees – we start to do special exercises. These have some effect, although we are still as flightless when we pass away as we always were. However, we have taken care to teach the exercises to our children who, throughout their lives, strive to improve and perfect them. They teach the exercises to their own children, and so on. After many generations, stumps start to show and – at some point in the far future – the wings are there again. People start to fly once more. I'm not sure exactly where the categories 'obstacle' and 'incapacity' might fit in at various points in the story, but this looks like a tale of *liberation* to me. Finally, the negativism favoured by libertarians is, perforce, sceptical of accounts of repression and liberation which juxtapose the way people are against the way people might be – of Marxian accounts of alienation, for example.[3] The legend questions this scepticism, as it ought to. After all, our capacity for such juxtaposition is fairly deep-seated. It is what makes us different from bees.

It only remains to add that there is nothing much new about the fantasy that humans can be transformed into insects, or serve as components in some well-oiled, smoothly running machine. How could there be when it appeals so forcefully to those who aspire to control? The ruthless will always seek the simple, all-embracing solution. Nor is there anything particularly right- or left-wing about the fantasy. Thus, for an especially gross and deluded example, one need only leaf randomly through *Mein Kampf* to come across the repeated assertion that 'The state is a means to an end', that 'Its end lies in the preservation and advancement of a community of physically and psychically homogeneous creatures' (1969: 357). Or, from someone more likeable, consider Peter Kropotkin, the early anarchist for whom 'The course traced by the modern philosophy of evolution' is supposed to do the trick. According to Kropotkin, the anarchist thinker 'merely considers society as an aggregate of organisms trying to find out the best way of combining the wants of the individual with those of cooperation for the welfare of the species' (1970: 47). Abolish the state, let evolution take hold, *et voila!* Aldous Huxley was right, in *Brave New World*, to satirise this way of conceiving the 'social problem' – the 'new totalitarianism' as he called it – by pointing out that the only way to really solve it is through the use of genetic engineering; in other words by transforming the human species into some quite different species (1946: 12).

It is beginning to look as if the libertarian story according to which the market supplies the single all-embracing solution to our problems is just one more version of this fantasy; that it is, if you like, an ideology for insects but not for humans. But a political philosophy ought to have some sort of connection with the way people really are. Libertarian readers will no doubt be quick to respond that this imputation is unfair, and in a way it is. But in order to rebut the charge, here is what libertarians have to do: they have to show that the market, left to itself, is the best device for social co-ordination that we have *while at the same time* recognising the essential, inescapable, separateness of persons, the fact that we each have our own lives to lead and that our plans can come into conflict as we, each of us, pursue them. This is the reconciliation libertarianism attempts, but with what success? That is the question I will now go on to consider.

Part II

Whenever I thought of you I couldn't help thinking of a particular incident which seemed to me very important. You and I were walking along the river towards the railway bridge and we had a heated discussion in which you made a remark about 'national character' that shocked me by its primitiveness. I then thought: what is the use of studying philosophy if all that it does for you is to enable you to talk with some plausibility about some abstruse questions of logic, etc., and if it does not improve your thinking about the important questions of everyday life, if it does not make you more conscientious than any . . . journalist in the use of the *dangerous* phrases such people use for their own ends.

Ludwig Wittgenstein, letter to Norman Malcolm (Malcolm 1958: 39)

Chapter 7

Moralising the market

In the case of the typical, or 'standard', human the ratio of brain volume to body size is vastly greater than in the case of any other known creature. This feature is no doubt intimately connected with our bipedality. The arms are left free to manipulate tools and other objects, an ability further facilitated by the opposable thumb. There is, almost certainly, an equally intimate connection between these features and still further facts; that humans can speak, write, reason, act intentionally. So far, so good; but, according to a view of the world popular with many libertarians, there is yet another characteristically human feature less frequently mentioned in textbooks of zoology. According to that view the human child is born, not just with the usual array of organs – brain, thumb, and so on – but with its own personal set of moral ('human', 'natural' or 'fundamental') *rights*. The existence of such rights is not so easily verified by routine post-natal medical examination, so it is worth asking how, if at all, it can be established.

In what follows, I shall focus upon just one argument, according to which the existence of moral rights can be inferred from the failings of any strict *consequentialism*. That argument will be very familiar to many readers – in some cases boringly so, thanks to its widespread influence – and there is already a gigantic literature devoted to its discussion.[1] Nevertheless, I ought to rehearse it here. I shall try to be brief.

Consider the following examples. There is a riot going on and many will die unless it is stopped fast. The sheriff picks an innocent bystander at random and shoots him dead. As a result, the mob is cowed and returns quietly home. Or: street violence is rife. It is impossible to catch the real criminals, so the authorities round up a number of innocent people and 'punish' them horribly with great publicity. After that, the violence stops. Or: you lend me £100, and I promise to pay you back next week. But, realising that you have no special need for the money, I give it to a desperately cold and hungry tramp instead. Or: the economy is in recession, and many will suffer, even starve, unless something is done. To this end, a minority of the population is rounded up, put in special camps, and forced to work very hard for nothing. As a result, the economy booms and the crisis is averted.

For all these cases (as for the many parallel examples to be found in more recent texts on ethics): (1) an *end* which is patently, uncontroversially good – stopping a riot, cutting violent crime, the relief of suffering, the promotion of the majority's well-being – is achieved by *means* which are self-evidently bad if not plain evil. Moreover, (2) for all we know it may be that the evil means are the only ones available for achieving the good end in these cases, there being no conveniently available device for ruling this possibility out in advance from among the great range of situations the world can throw up. It follows, as a first conclusion, that no consequentialist doctrine – that is, no ethical doctrine which prioritises the good end, thereby relegating means to a secondary status – can logically avoid the advocacy of evil means to achieve good ends in certain circumstances. (The most well-known version of consequentialism is, of course, utilitarianism, according to the 'classical' version of which 'the greatest good is the greatest happiness of the greatest number'.)

But, further, since there clearly can be such a thing as a good end (if not, perhaps, a 'greatest good'),[2] the question is raised of how to describe in more general terms what on earth could be wrong with sometimes maltreating the innocent few in order to benefit the great majority. The answer, or so the argument invites us to conclude, is that, (3) 'using' some to benefit others ignores the fact that we are, each of us, separate persons, each with a separate life of his or her own to lead. Considered from the moral standpoint, we are thus, in Kant's phrase, 'ends in ourselves'[3] and we each have a claim to be respected as such. Finally, (4), or so the argument stresses, the same point can be rephrased in terms of rights, for to have a right is to have a claim against others that they should respect you by treating you in certain ways and not in others. So it is held to follow, as a second conclusion, that no consequentialist ethic can successfully account for *the fact* that persons have rights.

The foregoing 'anti-consequentialist argument for moral rights', as I shall call it, is certainly persuasive. One would have to be a sort of moral idiot not to appreciate the evil in misusing the innocent, say, or the force of the obligation to keep promises. For anyone of ordinary moral sensibility, such facts are the data from which the argument derives its power. By appealing to these, and by throwing a certain implication of consequentialism into relief, it compels one to recognise that the existence of rights is also a moral fact.

However, the degree of support which the argument can draw from within philosophy at present is only partly explained by its persuasiveness, for there is also the enormous influence wielded by John Rawls's *A Theory of Justice* (1972) to consider. On its appearance, Rawls's book was described – not inaccurately – by the *Times Literary Supplement* (5 May 1972) as 'the most notable contribution to that tradition [of English-speaking political philosophy] to have been published since Sidgwick and Mill' (quoted in Daniels 1974: xii), and the 'contractualist' account of justice it outlines is specifically designed to rectify the failing in utilitarianism identified by the anti-consequentialist argument. Thus, for Rawls, 'The striking feature of the utilitarian view of justice is that it does not matter, except indirectly,' how a 'sum of satisfactions is distributed among individuals' and, as he summarises the position:

> Justice denies that the loss of freedom for some is made right by a greater good shared by others. The reasoning which balances the gains and losses of different persons as if they were one person is excluded. Therefore in a just society the basic liberties are taken for granted and the rights secured by justice are not subject to political bargaining or to the calculus of social interests.
>
> (1972: 28)

When one bears all this in mind – the argument's persuasiveness plus Rawls's influence – there can be little wonder that Nozick should have felt so confident about opening *Anarchy, State, and Utopia* (1974) with the unsupported assertion that:

> Individuals have rights, and there are things no person or group may do to them (without violating their rights).
>
> (1974: ix)

For all I know, Nozick may well have felt that the work necessary to underpin this claim had already been done for him by Rawls and others, and who could possibly have blamed him? But let us now note that there are great differences between Rawls's 'contractualist' account of justice and Nozick's libertarianism. On the one hand, Rawls (as is well known) argues for the recognition of two principles of justice; most notably, so far as the subject of this book is concerned, for a 'difference principle' according to which 'social and economic inequalities are to be arranged so that they are . . . to the greatest benefit of the least advantaged' (1972:

83). This clearly commits Rawls to the advocacy of a version of a 'redistributivist' welfare state in which the relatively more advantaged are made to contribute (through taxation, for example) to the relatively less advantaged until a point is reached at which the principle is satisfied. Nozick, on the other hand, after having asserted that individuals have rights, goes on to claim – with equal confidence – that 'So strong and far-reaching are these rights that they raise the question of what, if anything, the state and its officials may do', the implication he draws being that there is *hardly anything* that the state and its officials may do. For Nozick, only a 'minimal state, limited to the narrow functions of protection against force, theft, fraud, enforcement of contracts, and so on, is justified' because 'any more extensive state will violate persons' rights not to be forced to do certain things' (1974: ix).

The contrast between these conclusions is – or so I should think – quite sufficient to show that the anti-consequentialist argument leaves an awful lot open; that while it may convincingly demonstrate that we have rights *of some sort* it carries little information concerning what rights we have or even when it is that those rights count. (They may not always.) The point here, of course, is that libertarians – *some* libertarians at least – interpret the notion of a fundamental moral right in a particular way. For this type of libertarian, the moral order is realised in the world once it becomes the case that for each person, each person's fundamental rights are recognised and respected by all others. Moreover, this type of libertarian holds that the absolute right to own private property, and to dispose of it at will, is itself a fundamental right; and so, if this ethical position were correct, it would enable the libertarian to moralise the market, and so escape some of the objections I raised much earlier on. (For example, the 'rights' criterion rules out as unacceptable cases in which thieves offer to return stolen objects at a price.)[4] It would also supply the libertarian with a justification for the market which recognises our separateness as persons and thereby avoids the risk of reducing us to bee level.

The libertarian is helped in this strategy by the fact that it is possible to think of a working free market economy as itself a structure of rights. The latter are obviously not moral rights, of course, so much as 'positive', legally enforceable property rights, but there is something appealingly neat and aesthetically satisfying in the libertarian attempt to portray these as the nearest thing there can be on Earth to a reflection of the higher, or 'true', moral order, in the view that the Platonic Form of the Good is, so to speak, discernible between the lines of small print at the foot of any title deed. I shall now go on to examine this 'rights-based' (or deontological) version of libertarianism. I shall concentrate especially on the work of its most philosophically sophisticated proponent, Nozick, and I shall argue that, although persons undoubtedly have rights, supporters of the free market can, in reality, derive little comfort from the fact.

Finally, though – and in line with the over-broad but not entirely bland generalisation that ethical theories tend to be either rights-based or consequentialist in thrust – we must not lose sight of the fact that there is an alternative version of libertarianism according to which it is of less significance that humans possess rights than that they are the possessors of knowledge. The fact is hard to deny, of course, as is the further fact – upon which this other type of libertarianism also insists – that the sum of human knowledge is so vast that no one individual could possibly possess more than a minuscule portion of it; a consideration which becomes particularly evident when one bears in mind that 'knowledge' must include, not just 'propositional' knowledge but 'practical' knowledge or skill as well. The view in question moralises the market by arguing that the free market economy is the only system which respects such facts, and is thus the only system conducive to human flourishing. According to this view, the market is akin to the gene pool, and no less vital to the survival of the species.

For the crucial difference between these approaches compare Hayek's (consequentialist) claim that the slightest interference with the free market inevitably *leads*, in time, to 'serfdom' with Nozick's (rights-based) remark that 'Taxation of earnings from labor is *on a par with* forced labor' (1974: 169). For Nozick, the horror is with us already. It manifests its presence each time a millionaire is taxed a penny. Let us now consider this.

Chapter 8

Rights, wrongs and rhetoric

This is as good a point as any at which to remark that the modern, anti-consequentialist argument for the existence of rights is quite different from Locke's. The latter works rather backhandedly by inferring the existent from the non-existent. There being 'nothing more evident, than that creatures of the same species and rank, promiscuously born to all the same advantages of nature, should also be equal one amongst another without subordination or subjection' (Locke 1988: 269), reason is held to teach all who will but consult it 'that, being all equal and independent, no one ought to harm another in his Life, Health, Liberty, or Possessions' (ibid.: 271). The presence of rights is thus held to follow from there being no good evidence for their absence.[1] In contrast to Locke, the modern argument rests, as we have seen, upon an appeal to *the moral sense*. If you don't agree, or just can't recognise, that it is morally wrong to use some for the good of others (as in cases where the innocent are 'punished') then the argument will carry no force, at least not for you. (It is likely that Locke – the author of a celebrated polemic against the doctrine of innate knowledge – would have disapproved (1964 Book I: Chapter 3).)

1 ON ARGUMENTS FROM INTUITION

However, the core anti-consequentialist argument is *not* an 'argument from intuition', at least not straightforwardly so. It is important to get this straight from the outset, because so much of the case for rights-based libertarianism – the superstructure libertarians erect upon the core, in other words – rests upon appeals to intuition. There are other, subsidiary reasons too. One is that the use of such appeals is so widespread (as even a cursory glance through the pages of any recent journal of philosophical ethics will show). It is arguable that the responsibility, even for this, can be traced to Rawls's doorstep. According to Rawls – who, as usual, has some interesting things to say on the subject – moral philosophy aims to formulate principles which 'match our considered judgements'. A little later he describes his work as 'a theory of the moral sentiments' (1972: 48, 51). These are remarks likely to mislead those who neglect to read *A Theory of Justice* carefully enough.

Even so (and Rawls apart) it ought to go without saying that arguments from intuition have their dangers. At any rate, the sorts of arguments which normally tend to be categorised as such do. After all, the history of thought yields enough casualties with which to illustrate the point. These range from the eminent – such as Descartes, who thought an inner 'natural light of reason' to be the ultimate arbiter of truth – to the harmlessly bizarre, such as Lord Herbert of Cherbury (also seventeenth century), who held the existence of God and the necessity to worship him to be amongst the 'common notions . . . which it is not permissible to dispute' because 'It is in these notions . . . that we see a gleam of the Divine Wisdom' (Willey 1934: 116). A notable nineteenth-century example is provided by Dr William Whewell, whose reputation survives largely thanks to his having been mercilessly castigated by John Stuart Mill for holding that divorce should be illegal, as well as for his view – as Mill describes it – that 'reverence for superiors, even when personally undeserving, and obedience to existing laws, even when bad' are amongst the most sacred duties (1987: 269).

As a Victorian, it is hardly surprising that Whewell should have been imbued with Victorian values, but a century and a half later his claim that these positions can be derived from intuitively known, *a priori* principles is scarcely credible; and that is the point, of course. Intuitionist doctrines such as those mentioned rest on the presupposition that the truth of a proposition is revealed by its power to withstand the inspection of some (supposed) inner mental light, or perhaps to evoke some gut-feeling of conviction that things *must* be a certain way. This means that they can supply no plausible criterion for distinguishing genuine truth from mere dogmatic prejudice. (Why should your intuition that some proposition, *p*, must be true be any better than mine that *p* must be false?) It is not just an accident that, within moral philosophy, intuitionists have generally tended to be conservative – for authority and against change – and Mill's comment on Whewell that 'feeble arguments can easily pass for convincing when they are on the same side as the prevailing sentiment' is apt (1987: 270).

With this in mind, it is clearly worth asking whether the modern argument, powerful though it may initially appear, is really any better. May it not be a 'prevailing sentiment' dressed up as an argument? (Isn't talk of 'human rights' and their 'violation' an important part of every would-be respectable politician's ready-to-hand argot these days?) The answer is that there is much more to the argument than this, because it is not an argument from intuition in the manner of Descartes, Lord Herbert or Whewell at all. Its power does not lie in its capacity to withstand exposure to some 'moral sense' or 'inner light', but rather in what it forces the utilitarian to *throw overboard* if utilitarianism is to be preserved.

Let me elaborate the point, beginning with the observation that, whatever its drawbacks, one great attraction of utilitarianism is, undoubtedly, that it provides a device for sorting intuitions out. Any bundle of intuitions (convictions, moral 'feelings', call them what you like) will, no doubt, contain some which contradict others; and this will be all the more likely where the intuitions of more than one person are involved. One attraction of the consequentialist 'principle of utility' is that it functions as a sort of filter through which only rationally justifiable intuitions are allowed to pass ('rationally justifiable' meaning, for the classical utilitarians, in conformity with the greatest happiness). Now it is quite often quite clearly desirable to have some filtering device such as this at one's disposal (even if not exactly the principle of utility). The point, as Mill put it, is 'whether we ought to take the feelings as we find them . . . or whether the tendency of actions to promote the greatest happiness affords a test to which the feelings of morality should conform' (1987: 234). In Whewell's case there is absolutely no good reason for taking his feelings as we find them, if only because there is no good reason for thinking them to carry special authority just because they happen to be *his* feelings rather than someone else's. Morality loses little and gains much where the conceitedly overbearing holders of such 'intuitively' founded prejudices are forced into the open to argue the toss in accordance with an independent standard. The principle of utility does precisely this.

So far – and for utilitarianism – so good. But now note that it is just as logically open to the utilitarian to deal with the type of example upon which the core anti-consequentialist argument rests – in which unspeakable things are done in order to achieve good ends – in exactly the same way. Not that the utilitarian need deny sharing the feelings, or 'intuitions', the examples call up, but even these can be dismissed as 'mere' feelings or irrational prejudices on the grounds that they do not square with the principle of utility. But now consider what the utilitarian is forced to deny in order to preserve the principle of utility against the anti-consequentialist argument here; namely that, for example, there is always something wrong with victimising the innocent, or with slavery, or that one is usually under some sort of obligation to keep promises. To see the power of the argument it is only necessary to appreciate that to deny these is to deny claims which fall into an entirely different and more serious category from, say, Whewell's concerning the sanctity of marriage or reverence for superiors.

Where is the difference? In common with many who write on this subject, I think the answer has a lot to do with what Ronald Dworkin calls 'equal concern and respect for persons'. As Dworkin puts it, to show 'concern' is to treat people 'as human beings who are capable of suffering and frustration' and to show 'respect' is to treat them 'as human beings who are capable of forming and acting on intelligent conceptions of how their lives should be lived' (1977: 272). In my view, it is the presence or absence of this – or at least of something more or less adequately captured by the way Dworkin puts it here – which distinguishes the moral attitude from others. To think or act morally – as opposed to, say, selfishly, prudentially or instrumentally – *is* to show 'concern and respect' for the persons likely to be affected. It is this idea, or at least a similar idea, which Kant attempted to capture with his 'categorical imperative'. 'Act in such a way', he wrote, 'that you always treat humanity, whether in your own person or in the person of any other, never simply as a means, but always at the same time as an end' (1948: 96).

For future reference, and because Nozick wouldn't find the point especially congenial, note that this does not – as it stands – rule out 'using' or 'sacrificing' others for some given end. All it does is distinguish between types of attitude. In fact, the sheriff who showed equal concern and respect, or treated people as 'ends in themselves', might well end up shooting an innocent bystander to stop a riot just the same. Nevertheless, there is quite an important difference between this sheriff and the sheriff who is a pure utilitarian, if such a thing is really possible. It is that the former will realise that he is faced with a moral problem, a dilemma; he may do what he thinks best in the circumstances, but he will still feel that there is 'something wrong'. By contrast, the utilitarian sheriff won't. For the latter, the principle he applies will automatically yield the result that the victim just does not count.

So, there is a difference at issue; a difference between two sets of distinctions. On the one hand, there are distinctions to be drawn, as it were, *within* morality; between differing moral opinions or viewpoints, or between differing 'moralities'. On the other, there is the distinction between the moral attitude and others; between, if you like, morality and *amorality*. Thus, it seems to me that, had Mill ever managed to force Whewell out of his intuitionist cupboard and into the fresh air, they might have conducted quite an interesting argument in consequentialist terms while at the same time maintaining respect for persons. A present-day

Whewell might claim, for example, that watching violent movies on TV causes people to go out and commit violent acts themselves. A present-day Mill might deny that there is evidence for this. Neither would be denying that people count. Similarly, Islamic polygamy and Western monogamy are aspects of different moralities. There are, no doubt, interesting and broadly consequentialist explanations for their differences, and it may also be possible to argue their respective merits along such lines, but neither reduces persons to the status of mere tools or instruments.[2] But strict (or 'simpleminded') utilitarianism does, or at least it does for some people.

So, if this is right, we now have an explanation for the power of the core argument; namely that it is impossible to reject that argument without stepping right outside morality and judging things from an amoral standpoint. Call it an 'argument from intuition' if you like, but bear in mind that the 'intuitions' upon which it rests are intuitions which, as I put it earlier, only a 'moral idiot' could ignore. This type of moral idiot would be unable to distinguish between, say, sacrificing someone for the greater good (to avert a war, say) and sacrificing someone for the *fun* of the majority. Therefore, whereas it is frequently appropriate for the utilitarian to force 'intuitively founded' opinions to undergo an independent test, there is no way in which the utilitarian can do the same for – say – the prohibition against misusing the innocent without moving beyond the pale to take an amoral stance.

Let us now consider whether there is anything so persuasive to be said for pro-free market, rights-based libertarianism. Just to recap, the upshot of the discussion so far is that there are arguments from intuition and, on the other hand, arguments from intuition; so that one should take care to determine the precise nature of any 'intuition' before founding an argument upon it. Rights-based libertarianism frequently rests its case on (alleged) intuitions of one sort or another, and perhaps it is nothing more than a 'feeble argument' which only manages to pass as convincing because it happens to be 'on the same side as the prevailing sentiment'. As I shall now argue, there is little else to be said for it.

2   RIGHTS AND FENCES

2.1   What the Samaritan didn't do

The parable of the Good Samaritan also draws upon, and conjures up, some fairly powerful moral feelings (or 'intuitions'). As a way of getting to grips with the libertarian account, let us first remind ourselves of what the Samaritan did before turning to the more interesting question of what he didn't do. Let me add (quickly) that I am not trying to push a sermon here or to found an argument on an appeal to religion. The point is simply that the parable of the Good Samaritan – like the core anti-consequentialist argument – relies for its appeal upon a moral 'intuition' which is hardly arbitrary.

But I shall return to that. First, I think it safe to assume that pretty well all readers will be aware that the story relates to a certain man who went down from Jerusalem to Jericho and fell among thieves, 'which stripped him of his raiment, and wounded him, and departed, leaving him half dead'. Unlike the priest and the Levite in the story, who both 'passed by on the other side', the Samaritan had compassion on the victim, went to him, and bound up his wounds. He 'set him on his own beast, and brought him to an inn, and took care of him'. The following morning, the Samaritan departed only after having first made sure that the victim's immediate needs could be financially provided for at the inn. These needs were apparently quite modest. ('He took out two pence'.)[3]

Now, it seems to me that the moral which it is most natural to draw from this story concerns two of its features in particular. There is, first, the fact that the thieves' victim is in a pretty bad way; 'half dead' no less. The Samaritan does *not* give a handout to help finance some whim or luxury. (*Pace* an argument to which we shall be turning shortly, he does not deploy his undoubted skills as a hairdresser to supply the man in the ditch with a free haircut.) He caters to a desperate, immediate and evident need. Second, the Samaritan does nothing saintly or superogatory. For example, he does *not* rescue the man from a blazing building on the point of collapse, or dive into a stormy sea. In no way does he put himself at risk and nor, for that matter, is there any evidence in the story to suggest that the Samaritan has a pressing engagement of his own to keep, any appointment which it would be to his detriment to miss. In the light of these features, the natural moral to draw is that the Samaritan simply does what is expected of him. Whereas the priest and Levite are *to blame* for passing by, the Samaritan acts as any ordinary person ordinarily ought to in the situation described; and that, indeed, is the moral we are invited to draw. Christ's question to the disciples is, 'Which now of these three, thinkest thou, was neighbour unto him that fell among thieves?'; and neighbourliness is, I take it, quite a way distant from saintliness.

To generalise, if the priest and the Levite are at fault, and the Samaritan does nothing morally special, then the Samaritan only does what he ought to; so much so that he is morally *required* to do it; that is, he has a moral obligation. Finally – this being the case and rights being the issue here – let us note that, although one doesn't have to, it wouldn't be stretching things at all to put the point in terms of rights. One can put it in one or the other (though not both) of two alternative ways. One can say either, first, that the victim has a right to expect help from the Samaritan, corresponding to the Samaritan's duty to supply it, or else, second, that although the Samaritan would be 'acting within his rights' were he to ignore the victim and pass by on the other side, the fact is neither here nor there. Thanks to the overwhelming obligation, it would be wrong of the Samaritan to act within his rights.

2.2 Rights and fences

Rights-based libertarianism, consistently applied, must portray the story differently, and draw conclusions which are at odds with those which, as I think, it is natural to draw. Not that the libertarian need deny that the Samaritan does a good deed, or acts well, or even that the Levite and priest are at fault in neglecting to help. Libertarians can stress that morally better, or just plain nicer, people would stop, but that is about the only point of agreement between the libertarian and the 'natural' interpretations here. Otherwise, the libertarian has to claim that the victim has no right to be helped; that, because the Samaritan has a perfect right to pass by on the other side, he is under no obligation to help the victim. That, in other words, the Samaritan has no duty to help. All this conflicts with the 'natural' interpretation according to which, as we have seen, even if the Samaritan does have a right to pass by it is overridden or cancelled out by his obligation to help the victim. In short, the libertarian interpretation differs from the natural in that the libertarian does not have to describe the Samaritan's behaviour as morally required.[4]

So how is it that, as I am claiming, libertarianism is constrained to portray the story in this way? The answer is that libertarianism represents moral, or 'natural', rights in a certain way, with the help of a certain model or metaphor. The way libertarians portray the world, it is as if each of us were surrounded by his or her own personal invisible fence. According to this view, we act within our rights provided that we each remain within the perimeter it defines, and the fence is constructed out of the rights themselves. Others violate, or 'invade', our rights when they cross the fence without our permission or when, as Nozick puts it, 'Voluntary consent opens the border for crossings' (1974: 58). In the following passage, Nozick makes his reliance upon this metaphor strikingly explicit.

A line (or hyper-plane) circumscribes an area in moral space round an individual. Locke holds that this line is determined by an individual's natural rights, which limit the action of others. Non-Lockeans view other considerations as setting the position and contour of the line.

(1974: 57)

Nozick – who considers himself a Lockean – goes on to consider when, if at all, it is permissible to 'transgress the boundary'; and this talk of 'border-crossings' and 'boundary-crossings' recurs throughout *Anarchy, State, and Utopia*. It also underlies his well-known 'side-constraint view' of morality which 'forbids you to violate these moral constraints in the pursuit of your goals' (1974: 29). Nozick's view, as one might expect, is that rights can *only* function as side-constraints. Even the 'utilitarianism of rights', where 'some condition about minimising the total (weighted) amount of violations of rights is built into the desirable end-state to be achieved' is ruled out (1974: 28). He adds

Side constraints upon action reflect the underlying Kantian principle that individuals are ends and not merely means; they may not be sacrificed or used for the achieving of other ends without their consent. Individuals are inviolable.

(1974: 30–1)

So, within Nozick's picture of the world the moral life resembles a stroll through suburbia. You may pursue any goal you wish provided that you stick to the footpath and take no shortcut across anyone else's lawn. It is clearly consistent with this *Weltanschauung* that Nozick should hold, as he does, that only *consent* can license the crossing of a moral boundary. Where 'individuals are inviolable' in the sense of being sovereign possessors of moral territory, how could things be otherwise? Let me put it another way. I realise that talk of 'respect of persons' with their 'own' lives to lead lends itself to talk in terms of 'personal spaces' surrounded by 'boundaries' and so on. But, then, as I have previously argued, so does talk of laws as 'constraints' lend itself to the metaphor of obstacles and barriers. Just as negativist accounts of freedom tend to take this latter metaphor too seriously, so Nozick has allowed himself to be seduced into interpreting the 'territory' metaphor more seriously than he should.

To return to the Good Samaritan story, it should – or so I think – be equally clear how this picture of the moral world commits the libertarian to interpreting the parable in the way I have already outlined; for, on the libertarian view, the Samaritan has to reach out across his rights fence to help the victim. This may not be exactly saintly, but it is certainly beyond the call of duty and not morally required. The Samaritan is – as Nozick would put it – 'entitled' to remain within the boundary. Likewise, the priest and the Levite are perfectly entitled to stay on their own territory, and the poor victim certainly has no right (or 'entitlement') to be helped by any of the other characters, as this would involve reaching across, and maybe even trespassing onto the territory enclosed within, the rights-fences of others. Notice, too, that, on the 'natural' interpretation, the Samaritan's obligation to help (like the victim's right to be helped, if there is one) arises from the situation in which he finds himself. If it hadn't been that he just happened to be passing and in a position to help the obligation would not exist. If, for example, some third party had been passing instead, there would have been no right on the part of the victim to get that person to summon the Samaritan from his bed at midnight. On the contrary, it would then have been up to the third party to do what the Samaritan in fact did. This is also at odds with the libertarian view according to which rights-bubbles enclose persons like skin. Nozick thinks that 'individuals in combination cannot create new rights which are not the sum of preexisting ones' (1974: 90). How could he not when spontaneously growing a new skin is so difficult?

In summary, rights-based libertarianism assumes that *entitlements always take priority*.[5] It should be easy to see how this libertarian vision lends itself to a defence of the free market. Where each individual is portrayed as sovereign over his or her specific rights-'territory' it would be difficult not to portray absolute rights to private ownership over specific items as a subset of fundamental moral or 'natural' rights; and that, indeed, is how libertarians do portray property rights. The libertarian's moral prioritisation of consent obviously reflects, at a supposedly more fundamental level, the market exchange. Therefore, it is no exaggeration at all to claim, as I did earlier, that, for the libertarian, the capitalist free market is the nearest thing there can be on Earth to the realisation of the ultimate moral order.

Note also how the rights-fence model lends itself to the defence of a 'pure' capitalism here; an order in which the right to private property is *absolute*. This contrasts with real life. Where some version or other of the market actually operates, property rights are defined variously and compromised in all sorts of ways. As Mill pointed out, 'powers of exclusive use and control are very various, and differ greatly in different countries and in different states of society' (1976: 354); a point taken up more recently, and more painstakingly, by Lawrence Becker. Becker notes that the 'right to property' can include a large number of rights including (but not only) the rights to use, to manage, to derive income from, to consume, and to sell or bequeath, and that a combination of only some of these can constitute what is recognisably a right of ownership (Becker 1977: 18ff). Libertarians rarely concern themselves with such niceties.[6]

So which version of the parable is correct? (Note that I have not come down in favour of one or the other – at least not so far.) Should we stick with the natural interpretation, or should we reject it in favour of the libertarian account? A good way to proceed would be to apply a filter test, utilitarian-style, and consider what one has to deny if one rejects the former; and it is here that I think readers will see the point of my having chosen to discuss the parable rather than just any old story or philosopher's example. It is one of the most famous parables there is, and I think it undeniable that, as a result, its influence has extended far beyond the confines of the Christian religion over a considerable period of time. It is one of the root myths of 'Western' (perhaps not only Western) morality, and for many people the principles it illustrates (according to the natural interpretation) embody part of the moral attitude itself. These principles show up in locations as diverse as Oliver Twist's asking for more and the tales of Robin Hood and Pretty Boy Floyd; and if those principles have become internalised as 'intuitions', there is a good explanation for the fact. In short, to reject the natural interpretation is to deny principles which, over millennia, have become foundational to the moral vision of millions of people. That's all one rejects; but then that's quite a lot.

Not that time necessarily confers sanctity, of course. It didn't in the case of slavery and, if feminists are to be believed, it doesn't in the case of 'patriarchy' either; but these conflict with the 'respect for persons' criterion, so there are good reasons for rejecting them which are absent in the case of the principles embodied by the natural interpretation of the parable. Nor are libertarians exactly wrong here. It is more that they are different. There is, I suppose one could say, a 'libertarian morality', just as there is a morality which endorses monogamy and another which endorses polygamy, but we should view this libertarian morality as a distortion of a more deeply entrenched moral framework.

Consider what this means. It means that it is inaccurate to treat rights-based libertarianism as a philosophical theory for which good arguments, with well-founded premises, can be produced. It is not that at all. It is more an exercise in rhetoric, an attempt to persuade us – for no very good reason – to change our moral vision and attitudes in favour of the alternatives it offers.

3 HEALTH AND HAIRCUTS

Anarchy, State, and Utopia supplies plenty of examples with which to illustrate the point, but it will be particularly useful here to consider Nozick's comments on a passage from Bernard Williams's article, 'The Idea of

Equality'. The article is, as Nozick says, 'influential'. Williams writes:

> Leaving aside preventive medicine, the proper ground of distribution
> of medical care is ill health: this is a necessary truth. Now in very many
> societies, while ill health may work as a necessary condition of receiving
> treatment, it does not work as a sufficient condition, since such treat-
> ment costs money, and not all who are ill have the money; hence the
> possession of sufficient money becomes in fact an additional necessary
> condition of actually receiving treatment. . . . When we have the situ-
> ation in which, for instance, wealth is a further necessary condition of
> the receipt of medical treatment, we can once more apply the notions
> of equality and inequality: not now in connection with the inequality
> between the well and the ill, but in connection with the inequality
> between the rich ill and the poor ill since we have straightforwardly the
> situation of those whose needs are the same not receiving the same
> treatment, though the needs are the ground of the treatment. This is an
> irrational state of affairs . . . it is a situation in which reasons are
> insufficiently operative; it is a situation insufficiently controlled by
> reasons – and hence by reason itself.
>
> (1969: 121)

Nozick interprets this passage as showing that Williams is making an
unfounded assumption. He comments:

> Williams seems to be arguing that if among the different descriptions
> applying to an activity, there is one that contains an 'internal goal' of
> the activity, then (it is a necessary truth that) the only proper grounds
> for the performance of the activity, or its allocation if it is scarce, are
> connected with the effective achievement of the internal goal. If the
> activity is done upon others, the only proper criterion for distributing
> the activity is their need for it, if any. Thus it is that Williams says (it is
> a necessary truth that) the only proper criterion for the distribution of
> medical care is medical need.
>
> (1974: 233–4)

Nozick questions this, and points out that, if it were right, it would be
equally true that 'the only proper criterion for the distribution of barbering
services would be barbering need'. But 'If someone becomes a barber
because he likes talking to a variety of different people, and so on, is it
unjust of him to allocate his services to those he most likes to talk to?'; or
what if 'he works as a barber in order to pay tuition at school' and only
chooses to cut the hair of those who pay or tip well (1974: 234)? On
Nozick's account, it seems pretty clear that there can be nothing unjust or

otherwise objectionable about the barber's choosing to allocate his services according to these criteria rather than Williams's criterion of need, and he asks 'In what way does the situation of a doctor differ?' Of course, the implication is meant to be that the respective situations of barber and doctor are no different, and that Williams's argument is flawed.

I should like to examine the mechanics of Nozick's objection to Williams in a little detail, so it will be helpful to set out its three main elements as follows:

Claim 1 (Williams's claim) The proper criterion for the distribution of health care between persons should be (the degree of seriousness of) their need for health care. Other criteria, such as differences in ability to pay, should not count.

Principle P For any activity with an internal goal, the proper criterion for deciding, between persons, upon who should benefit from the achievement of that activity's goal should be (the degree of seriousness of) their need to benefit from its being achieved. Other criteria, such as differences in ability to pay, should not count.

Claim 2 The proper criterion for the distribution of haircuts between persons should be (the degree of seriousness of) their need for a haircut. Other criteria, such as differences in ability to pay, should not count.

The issues are the truth or falsity of claim 1 and the assumption that principle *P* holds. Nozick's argument is that claim 1 presupposes principle *P* and, consequently, the truth of claim 2. Against this, he is pointing out that, since claim 2 is manifestly false, claim 1 must be false also.

3.1 Conflicting intuitions

I should like to comment on three aspects of the argument. The first is the way Nozick presents the difference between Williams and himself in terms of a straightforward conflict of reactive intuitions. Thus, Williams's claim is represented by Nozick as a brute prejudice. 'Despite appearances', he writes, 'Williams presents no argument for it'. Nozick also suggests that, although the claim is often asserted, there is no plausible argument for it. If there is, he writes 'I would like to see *that* argument set out in detail' (1974: 233) (emphasis in original). Likewise, Nozick relies upon his readers to find it plain obvious that claim 2 is false.

In fact, Williams is not just stating a prejudice and there is a great deal to be said in support of his position, but let us first take things on Nozick's terms. To begin with, let us observe that Nozick's 'New Right' attitude to haircuts (with which I am strongly in sympathy by the way) is one indicator of his difference from the 'Old Right', for many of whom haircuts are very important. If Nozick had attended an English public school in his youth he would know that, for some of them, 'Compulsory Haircuts for All!' can even assume the status of a fundamental moral axiom. So, there is the possibility that there can be individuals who might well favour a system which ensured that all who need haircuts get them, and who might even favour the use of coercive 'redistributive' measures to achieve this. This leads to the further observation that, because Nozick is arguing from intuition here, something hangs upon *whose* intuitions are being addressed.

Reactions can vary. For example, suppose we were to put Nozick's argument to some representative Old Right figure, Colonel Blimp, say, or – to bring things more up to date – Colonel Blimp's yuppie son. This person strongly favours the provision of haircuts for all who need them, but is also convinced that the lower orders should be left to fend for themselves so far as health care is concerned (i.e. that claim 1 is false whereas claim 2 is true). Assuming that principle *P* holds, we may use (a version of) Nozick's argument *either* to persuade this person to drop his prejudice in favour of haircuts (i.e. to persuade him that since claim 1 is false claim 2 must be false also) *or* to drop his prejudice against health care provision (i.e. to persuade him that claim 1 is just as true as claim 2). Or, alternatively, let us put Nozick's argument to a representative of the hard-nosed 'Old Left'. Call him – or her – 'Stalin'. 'Stalin' will of course favour the distribution of health care according to need and will also – thanks to his or her authoritarian temperament and general sympathy for a regimented totalitarianism – have a sneaking liking for the idea of the compulsory distribution of haircuts according to need. This person may well use Nozick's argument, or should I say a reverse version of it, to persuade others that claim 2 is just as true as claim 1.

Son-of-Blimp and 'Stalin' are comic-book caricatures of course (at least I hope they are), but we may draw upon their stylised reactions to loosen the hold of intuition here and to point out that Nozick's argument is less decisive than it might appear at first. As a libertarian, Nozick is confident that the first intuition – that claim 1 is true – *must* be the claim at fault, but why be so sure? So long as we remain content to rest arguments on gut-reactions or inner feelings there is no justification for being so positive.

Still, this isn't a great deal of help to those like me (and presumably Williams) who want to assert claim 1 while denying the truth of claim 2. Son-of-Blimp, 'Stalin' and Nozick all assume that claims are logically related – that there is a relation of mutual entailment between them – so that they stand or fall together. How can the claims be prised apart?

3.2 The naming of cats

This question brings us to a second feature of Nozick's argument: his use of principle *P* with which to connect claims 1 and 2. Recall that, according to the principle, for *any* activity with an internal goal, the proper basis for distribution is need. It is, thus, quite clear that Nozick's objection to Williams rests upon the following assumption.

For any *X* and any *Y* (*X* and *Y* being objects or states of affairs) where (i) *X* and *Y* share common features and, (ii) proposition *p* is true for *X*, *p* must also be true for *Y*.

Without this, Nozick would be unable to allege that claim 1 has a counter-intuitive implication, nor would he be able to argue back from claim 2's absurdity to claim 1's falsity. However, I doubt that the reader will find it too difficult to detect the flaw. The problem is that Nozick's assumption only holds for those propositions, *p*, whose truth is *a feature of* or *results from* those characteristics shared by *X* and *Y*. For example, suppose that *X* is a cat. If so, it will also be true, *p*, that '*X* is a member of the species *felis catus*', and there is no problem about making the logical inference from this to the conclusion that if *Y* is also a cat then it must be equally true of *Y* that it is a member of the same species. The assumption holds here.

But now consider a case where it does not. Suppose it is also true, *p*, that '*X* is called Tiddles'. There are plenty of other cats in the world, including *Y*, and all of them have plenty of characteristics in common with *X*. Are we to conclude that they are also called Tiddles; that we have been mistaken all along in our assumption that they had other names; 'Possum' or 'MacAvity'? Should we, perhaps, reject our initial 'intuitions' on this point? Of course not, because the names we happen to give cats do not flow logically or causally from those features by which they are rendered classifiable as cats.

Exactly the same goes for Nozick's argument. It is true that both medicine and hairdressing can be schematically presented as 'activities with an internal goal'. It is also true – as I hold – that the proper criterion for the distribution of medical care should be degree of need (claim 1); but I would only be committed to drawing the same conclusion for hairdressing *if* I thought the 'distribution according to need' criterion *followed*, in the case of medicine, from its being an activity with an internal goal. But I don't. On the contrary, I hold its appropriateness in the case of medicine to be connected with such factors as medicine's importance to life and the relative scarcity of medical expertise; i.e. *not* its 'goal directedness'.

As it happens, I have other convictions about medicine too. For example, I think that only qualified surgeons should be allowed to perform operations. Hairdressing, like medicine, is 'an activity with an internal goal', so should I conclude that only qualified surgeons should be allowed to cut hair? If Nozick were right, I should. And (since he holds the relation between claims 1 and 2 to be one of mutual entailment) I would also have to contradict myself, because I have no such scruples over hairdressing. So far as I am concerned, *anyone* should be allowed to cut hair. Medicine, like hairdressing, has an 'internal goal', so should I conclude that anyone, including my local barber, should be permitted to conduct heart by-pass surgery? Nozick's free market principles might enable him to hold this view, but it isn't mine, and I am, in any case, not committed to this conclusion by his argument.[7]

Nozick's choice of principle *P* with which to relate medicine and hairdressing is quite arbitrary and without foundation. He has no good reason for choosing *that* principle as opposed to some other. It follows, as I have been claiming, that its force is only rhetorical. It may be that, by placing Williams's position against a certain background, it makes that position look temporarily silly (to some), but that is all it does.

3.3 Context

Let us now turn – thirdly – to the strangely over-schematic manner in which Nozick presents his case. The way Nozick's arguments from intuition rely upon his readers to share certain (unacknowledged) presuppositions of context is quite interesting. Take your barber, for example. I mean your local, small-town, friendly neighbourhood barber. There he is, neatly installed in his modest, though clean, premises. As he works, he chats in a friendly and informal manner to some long-standing and valued customer, and – through snippets of conversation you overhear – you learn that, like many a good father, he is striving to pay for his children's schooling. Can't you just picture him on the cover of the *Saturday Evening Post*? Wouldn't you resent it if he were forced by some (no doubt 'faceless' and bureaucratic) authority to distribute his services according to some principle of need? *Of course* you would. But now suppose that things aren't like that. For example, suppose that in your area (i) all barbers are white and (ii) all barbers are racially prejudiced against blacks. Suppose this means that all barbers refuse to cut the hair of blacks. Maybe haircuts are less 'necessary' than health, but hygiene and comfort do, after a time, impose limits. The resulting situation could easily come to resemble the situation legitimated by the mean, petty and vindictive 'Jim Crow' race laws which used to prevail in the southern USA. Wouldn't you *then* favour the state's compelling barbers to distribute their services differently?

In conclusion, the root contradiction lying at the heart of Nozick's technique is that, while relying on such presuppositions of context, he disdains them at the same time, preferring to concentrate on abstracted, formal similarities between cases (such as the fact that both medicine and hairdressing are 'activities with an internal goal'). This can create the impression that Nozick is getting right down to the theoretical nitty-gritty – that, maybe, there is *real* philosophy going on here – but, in reality, it completely misses the point. It is our knowledge of the real world, together with the assumptions we make about it, which frequently conditions the moral judgements we make and which enables us to make the real distinctions which exist between the cases Nozick conflates. And what goes for the 'barber' example here goes for medicine too. If all known diseases could be cured by taking a single, cheap and easily available pill, then the judgements we made about how it is 'proper' for doctors to behave might be different. Unfortunately, the real world isn't like that.

3.4 How Nozick misinterprets Williams

So what does Nozick miss exactly? A brief consideration of this question will allow us to make a few positive observations in support of claim 1, as well as to note just how seriously Nozick misportrays Williams's argument through misreading his intentions.

Note, first, that Williams's remark that 'the possession of sufficient money' should not be 'an additional necessary condition of actually receiving treatment' echoes Aneurin Bevan's comment that 'A person ought to be able to receive hospital and medical help without being involved in financial anxiety' (*Hansard* 30 April 1946).[8] Bevan was the government minister primarily responsible for the introduction of the British National Health Service and in 1946 he was addressing Parliament on the subject. Williams is also British, and his article was originally published in 1962 which means that he could have taken the majority of his readership's support for the 'post-war consensus' in favour of the welfare state for granted. It is against this ideological background that we must place Williams's argument if we are to understand it accurately, and simply casting it in this light shows up how Nozick parodies it through what he omits to say.

For a start, and as Bevan makes clear, the principle at stake is that lack of finance should not be a barrier to the receipt of medical care; that is, that it is 'proper' that need should always override ability to pay when it comes to making sure that the sick are tended. It is not the principle that for all cases need should come first. The way Nozick puts it, you would think it to be Williams's view that – for example – where a cosmetic surgeon has to choose which of two vastly expensive 'nose jobs' to perform on some occasion, that surgeon should always treat the millionaire with the ugliest nose first and make the other wait. But the principle at issue is weaker and has no relevance to this type of case. Moreover, the National Health Service was a system of payments. Doctors were, as it were, reimbursed for treating those who would otherwise be unable to pay. So far as I know, no doctor was ever directly forced by these arrangements to apply the need principle. It is true, of course, that force was needed to make the system work, but a better analogy would be one in which taxpayers are forced to reimburse barbers for attending to the hair of the poor but needy. (Readers initially seduced by Nozick's appeals to intuition might like to consider whether they would object so strongly to that. Would they object if the measure were introduced to counteract the racism endemic amongst barbers?)

Second, we should note that Williams's avowed purpose is to explicate a certain ideal, the ideal of equal respect for persons. 'Equal treatment according to need' flows from this, and Williams's aim is to outline what one is committed to *where this ideal applies* or 'is invoked'. He has to be right to insist that *where* one invokes the ideal one must count 'external' factors, such as wealth, as irrelevant, but neither the ideal nor the inference need apply everywhere. Third, Williams quite plausibly connects respect for persons and equal treatment with a certain 'common humanity' which gives rise to moral claims through such 'very obvious human characteristics' as 'feeling pain and desiring affection' (1969: 114). The need for medical care is connected with such characteristics, just as 'the fact that a man is black is, by itself, quite irrelevant to the issue of how he should be treated in respect of welfare, etc' (1969: 113). Williams is saying – in short – that withholding health care on grounds of lack of wealth *is as bad as racism*. I strongly agree, and I would add that – obviously – so is the behaviour of racist barbers, although this has nothing to do with hairdressing's being 'an activity with an internal goal'. (As we have seen, Nozick chooses to illustrate his position, at one point, with an example featuring a real-life character who 'made it' from a humble ethnic minority background. But readers initially impressed by Wilt Chamberlain's success story – as told by Nozick, that is – or who feel inclined to agree with him that doctors, like barbers, should be free to refuse treatment to whomsoever they like, might care to reflect on the fate of Bessie Smith.)[9]

There is nothing at all arbitrary or taken for granted about any of this, and, fourth, Williams's position is further strengthened by the fact that, in the real world, doctors are so often placed in situations resembling the Samaritan's. This means that he can draw upon some fairly deep-rooted axioms of common morality for support. By contrast, the libertarians' revised version of the Bible would have to re-write the famous passage from the Book of Luke along the following lines: Two men were beaten up, robbed, and left for dead in a ditch. Along came a Samaritan who could have easily rescued both but didn't feel like it. The Samaritan said 'I will rescue the one who will offer me the highest price.' He was lucky. It turned out that one of the men was a millionaire who, after some hard bargaining, was persuaded to accompany the Samaritan to the nearest Hilton and treat the Samaritan, with ten of his friends, to a slap up meal and a night on the town. Who could blame the Samaritan for this? He was only acting within his 'entitlements'.

Somehow this lacks the conviction of the original.

4 DANGEROUS PHRASES

Let me just summarise the conclusions we have now reached. First, it is important to distinguish between the *core* anti-consequentialist argument for rights and the *libertarian superstructure* erected upon that core, which construes rights as invisible fences. Second, the latter is out of kilter with the moral standpoint it is often 'natural' to take, as a consideration of the Good Samaritan parable illustrates. Therefore, we need some very good reasons for rejecting it in favour of libertarianism. Third, the rejection of the libertarian view is consistent with the main conclusion established by the core argument; namely that respect for persons, for Kant's imperative never to treat another merely as a means, must be crucially embodied within any moral perspective. Indeed, Williams's 'welfare statist' view of the proper grounds for health care distribution is itself consistent with this conclusion, although it also stands in contradiction to libertarianism. Fourth, Nozick's use of the 'barber' example to persuade us of the reverse fails because the resemblances between that case and the case of health care upon which he chooses to focus are quite arbitrarily selected, and do not permit the logical inference he wants us to make from one case to the other.

To amplify the last point, Nozick's 'barber' argument exemplifies the following rhetorical technique: (1) Select some claim, *p*, preferably containing a dangerous, politically loaded, phrase – 'rights', 'human rights', 'human needs', 'justice', 'freedom', 'democracy', or whatever; (2) Select an example which resembles, in certain formal respects, the sort of situation to which p is normally thought to apply, having first made sure that the example is fairly trivial and absolutely *not* the sort of example to which it would normally be thought appropriate to apply p; (3) Assume that the formal resemblances between the serious and trivial cases permit inference from one to the other; (4) Conclude that p is false. As I have argued, the technique fails on the rational level, thanks to the falsity of assumption (3), but we should note that, where the 'serious' case is presented in the light of the 'trivial', we are – as weak and fallible humans – only too liable to *feel* the force of Nozick's conclusion; that is, to have what might be appropriately termed an 'intuition'. We should note further – as a fifth conclusion – that the intuition in question is bogus, although it is no doubt an intuition which those already prejudiced in favour of libertarianism are only too likely to have.

Nozick's main aim is to undermine the case for the welfare state, so things would be bad enough for his argument if it only failed at the point just under discussion. However, there are plenty of other crucial points in which it fails, in the same manner and for the same reason. In fact, it wouldn't be too much of an exaggeration to say that the technique just outlined *is* Nozick's technique. It is certainly worth remarking that he devotes a short chapter to its discussion; and that, in it, he mentions 'the difficulties in convincing someone to change his evaluation of a case by producing a parallel example' and the virtues of challenging someone to 'draw the line' (1974: 277–9). This is all very well, and has something to be said for it, but *not* where the 'parallel examples' can be easily distinguished in straightforward moral terms and are therefore patently not parallel from the outset.

Finally, as I am claiming that Nozick's argument fails because of his repeated use of this technique, I ought to bring this chapter to a close by giving a few more examples of the technique at work. I shall give four. Each comes at a crucial point in Nozick's discussion.

The first occurs in Chapter 5 of *Anarchy, State, and Utopia* where Nozick discusses H.L.A. Hart's 'principle of fairness'. According to Hart's formulation, 'when a number of persons conduct any joint enterprise according to rules and thus restrict their liberty, those who have submitted to these restrictions when required have a right to a similar submission from those who have benefited by their submission' (Hart 1955: 185). If viable, this principle can obviously be used to justify the state's right to levy taxes for the finance of public utilities, and it also presupposes that rights can arise where individuals are related in a given way in a given context, as in the Samaritan story but contrary to Nozick's own view. (Hart's view is closer to Locke's than the 'neo-Lockean' Nozick's. According to Hart 'there is at least one natural right, the equal right of all men to be free' (1955: 175). Other 'special' rights arise only in given contexts, in the case of 'joint enterprise' for example (1955: 185), and since 'to have a right entails having a *moral* justification for limiting the freedom of another person' (1955: 183), this means that the liberty of all must be restricted equally in such cases.) Against Hart's view, Nozick invites the reader to 'Suppose some of the people in your neighborhood . . . have found a public address system and decide to institute a system of public entertainment' and that 'they post a list of names, one for each day, yours among them. On his assigned day . . . a person is to run the public address system, play records over it' and so on. Nozick concludes that one would not be obliged to participate when one's turn comes (1974: 93).

This seems reasonable on the face of things, if only because Nozick is describing (though without actually saying so) a system of 'taxation without representation'. However, does it follow that the principle of fairness is flawed; that it cannot be used to justify, for example, taxation either? It seems to me that Nozick parodies Hart by misreading his intentions here, rather as he does with Williams. It depends whether the principle is meant to be necessary, though *not* sufficient, to establish a right to interfere with liberty (as in the case of taxation), or whether it is meant to be *both* necessary *and* sufficient. Hart makes it clear that he is taking the former view, that 'the moral justification for interference which is to constitute a *right* to interfere (as distinct from merely making it morally good or desirable to interfere) is restricted to certain special conditions' (Hart 1955: 190). Hart is tentative – 'I cannot myself yet show that this is so' (ibid.), he writes – but it can't be silly to suggest that the *extra* conditions required to justify interference are present in the case of taxation but absent in Nozick's bizarre example. However, Nozick takes Hart to be claiming that, for *any* situation in which individuals benefit from burdens borne by others – that is, with that particular set of abstracted formal features – the principle must apply. That would be absurd, but it is neither an interesting claim nor is it Hart's.

Second, consider the 'Wilt Chamberlain' case again. This popular and likeable star's rise to fame was rendered all the more difficult by his having to begin from a severely deprived background (or so I gather).[10] Given this, and the further fact that – as described in the example – he employs his talents for the innocent amusement of thousands on Saturday afternoons, who could reasonably claim (on *these* grounds) that Chamberlain's exercise of liberty 'upsets patterns'. Where the directors of major capitalist corporations, Wall Street money dealers and suchlike persons, exercise their liberty, this also upsets patterns, so shouldn't we conclude, as Nozick would like us to, that their activities or their consequences are just as unobjectionable? We should, but *only if* the relevant parameter permitting inference from Chamberlain's case to the case of capitalism is just that, for both, 'liberty upsets patterns' (which plays the role of principle, *P*, here); and only those already persuaded in favour of rights-based libertarianism are likely to swallow that.

Third, take Nozick's much discussed 'marriage market' example. Nozick asks us to suppose twenty-six women and twenty-six men each wanting to be married, and that, for each sex, every member ranks the members of the opposite group in the same order of preference. A and A' marry voluntarily, as do B and B', despite the fact that individuals have removed themselves from the pool. C and C' also marry voluntarily – and so on down the line. Even Z and Z', whose choices are severely limited marry voluntarily. We are supposed to conclude that 'similar considerations apply to market exchanges between workers and owners of capital'; that even a worker faced with the choice between badly paid and unpleasant work and starving chooses 'voluntarily' to work. And this would indeed follow if the only relevant point of comparison between the worker and the characters in Nozick's schematic example were that, for both, 'other people's actions place limits on . . . available opportunities' (1974: 262). This brings me, fourthly and as promised, to

Taxation of earnings from labor is on a par with forced labor.

(1974: 169)

Not that Nozick is wrong. On the contrary, Nozick's phrase 'on a par with' is too tentative. The hours you work in order to pay your taxes are hours in which you generate money which is forcibly taken from you by the state. If you don't pay your taxes, you can go to prison, so it is *just plain true* that, as Nozick says, those are hours in which your labour is forced labour. But the question this raises is, so what? Should the contemplation of this undoubted fact cause the sensitive heart to bleed? I think not. In any decently organised society the state will employ a system of progressive taxation to finance public goods such as health care, education and transport, and the more marginal the effect on the lifestyle of that system's 'victims' – the less it interferes with their ability to live well – the more difficult it becomes to feel sympathy.

Of course, 'forced labour' is not a phrase which immediately causes one to think of routine taxation; and especially not of the taxation of those who can well afford to be taxed. Its connotations are quite other than this (as I'm sure Nozick knows very well). The phrase is more likely to remind one of the sort of forced labour *system* employed by Stalin (the real Stalin this time). Under Stalin, rebellious peasants 'were organised in mammoth labour camps and employed in the building of canals and railways'. This soon 'degenerated into slave labour, terribly wasteful of human life'. Stalin also used the system to reduce men of the opposition 'to such miserable, animal-like existence that they should be incapable of the normal processes of thinking and of formulating their views' (I am quoting from Isaac Deutscher's much-praised biography, 1966: 335, 356).

In a modern Western economy with a welfare state, is it true that the wealthy (and not quite so wealthy) middle-class are organised into vast labour camps? Some of their taxes may go to pay for railways, but are they forced to build railways themselves? Are they reduced by taxation to a 'miserable, animal-like existence' which renders them incapable of normal thinking processes? Of course not, and it is easy enough to detect the same rhetorical technique at work here too. Thus, while it is true enough that both taxed middle-class labour and the labour of Stalin's slaves is, in an obvious sense, 'forced labour', it is difficult to see why *that* should be the point of comparison which permits the transfer of moral judgement between these cases. It plays the same role as 'is an activity with an internal goal' in the 'barber' case. Nozick's use of the phrase insinuates that taxation from earnings is almost as, if not just as, bad as Stalin-style forced labour, but there are plenty of obvious differences – the camps, the barbed-wire, the cold, the beatings, the casual attitude to death, the lousy food, the starvation, to mention a few – which suggest that the inference cannot be made. Moreover, Nozick's argument begs the question, because it will only appeal to those libertarians who are already convinced that taxation from earnings is as bad as forced labour (and who, thus, have the right 'intuitions'). Others may ignore it.

Chapter 9

Visions of Valhalla

Within the shadowy halls of the elect trading goes on as eternally usual. The gods and saints exchange entitlements, one for another, as they adjust things to suit day-to-day fluctuations in their needs and wants. We poor mortals who seek grace must strive to replicate the situation, imperfectly no doubt, but as well we can. At any rate, that is what libertarians would like us to believe. But, as we have seen, one need only chip away at the foundations a little to discover that there is nothing to shore up this rickety vision but an over-exaggerated metaphor. How characteristic of our times it is, though, that heaven should be pictured as Wall Street in the sky.

In this chapter, I should like to explore this theme further. There would be no point in any more detailed examination of Nozick's argument, because the view of rights rejected in the last chapter lies at the heart of this type of libertarianism's world picture. Other rights-based libertarians present less well-articulated accounts than Nozick's and, although some readers will no doubt feel that all hangs on some other argument, as Nozick says of Williams, I should like to see *that* argument set out in detail. I doubt that it exists, and it would now be more interesting to widen the discussion.

1 THE REALM OF TRUE FREEDOM

It is equally characteristic of our times, I guess, that so much libertarian theory should be couched in the technical style of post-war 'analytic' philosophy. Here too, Nozick provides a good example, with his piecemeal approach, his careful examination of (sometimes surprising and unusual) examples and counter-examples, his tendency to explore an argument's less obvious implications in detail, and so on. All of this is absolutely fine, but in the case of libertarianism – one of its more interesting aspects – the style of expression completely belies the content of the theory expressed.

The way rights-based libertarians handle the concept of freedom is one good illustration of the point. What I have in mind is this. One would expect analytically-inclined philosophers sympathetic to libertarianism to agree with Berlin that 'the belief that some single formula can in principle be found whereby all the diverse ends of men can be harmoniously realised is demonstrably false' (Berlin 1969: 169). One would expect them to hold the idea of any such 'realm of true freedom' to be a futile, not to say dangerous, illusion which can only be fostered with the help of some highly suspicious logical sleights of hand; and I am sure that, in their more sober moments, many of them will tell you just that. Are there not – moreover – freedom's myriad 'recognised antitheses' to consider, and wouldn't those sleights involve glossing over and distorting these? I think they would. But remove the analytically-styled packaging and you will find concealed within it just one more version of exactly this illusion.

In fact, it is surprising how *little* close attention the concept of freedom receives from libertarian writers. Once again, *Anarchy, State, and Utopia* is a case in point. The word 'freedom' doesn't even appear in the index. The word 'liberty' appears, but only to refer the reader to the 'Wilt Chamberlain' passage. In a supposedly 'libertarian' work, this is more than surprising. It is truly remarkable.

The explanation for this glaring oversight isn't hard to find however. It is that, contrary to their chosen *nom de guerre* libertarians aren't really interested in liberty that much. Their primary concern is to defend private property, and the result is that liberty only enters the argument at points where it can be conveniently *re-defined* in terms of private ownership. The 'rights as fences' metaphor is pivotal here too. For the libertarian, you are free provided that no one 'violates' or 'invades' your moral 'territory' (your 'personal space') by crossing your boundary or fence. Otherwise, you remain free provided that you stick to your own territory and – notice – it makes no difference how narrowly circumscribed that territory is. As we have already noted, 'facts of nature' do not limit freedom on this account; and, for Nozick, the rights of others are just as 'natural' as gravity, so that even poor Z and Z' in the 'marriage market' case must be said to marry 'voluntarily'. Likewise, you limit another's freedom only when you trespass across that person's fence and invade his or her territory. Still, there is no need to tease this presupposition from between Nozick's lines when it is stated quite explicitly by Rothbard, in the following passage for example.

We are now in a position to see how the libertarian defines the concept of 'freedom' or 'liberty'. Freedom is a condition in which a person's ownership rights in his own body and his legitimate material property are *not* invaded, are not aggressed against. A man who steals another man's property is invading and restricting the victim's freedom, as does the man who beats another over the head. Freedom and unrestricted property right go hand in hand. On the other hand, to the libertarian, 'crime' is an act of aggression against a man's property right, either in his own person or his materially owned objects. 'Slavery' – the opposite of freedom – is a condition in which the slave has little or no right to self-ownership; his person and his produce are systematically expropriated by his master by the use of violence.

(Rothbard 1973: 41)

This may be 'how the libertarian defines' the concept of freedom, but a definition of 'freedom' it is not.[1] To call it a definition of 'freedom' is like calling the 'Ministry of Propaganda' the 'Ministry of Truth'. For a start, let us note that slavery is not *the* opposite of freedom. Slavery is *an* opposite of freedom; just one of freedom's many 'recognised antitheses' (in Austin's phrase). Others – already noted – are the presence of an obstacle sufficient to prevent an action, subjection to the will of another, coercion. Of course, it would suit the libertarian very well to assimilate these to slavery, because to hold the status of slave really is, by definition, to be the property of another person; but it is a rather long jump from this to the conclusion that, *for all cases* of freedom and its violations, definitions of the relevant terms must presuppose property rights of the sort presupposed by capitalism.

Moreover, it is a relatively straightforward matter to demonstrate that they do not. The sheer *chutzpa* with which Rothbard denies the obvious – the brassed-facedness of it all – beggars belief. On the one hand, it is easy to think up counter-examples to Rothbard's definition in the form of cases where no one's rights are violated but someone's freedom obviously is. For example, the prisoner has been found guilty. (He really is guilty.) The judge sentences the prisoner, and – being a judge – he has a right to do this. 'Take him down!' says the judge. Two burly warders grab the prisoner – as they have a right to – and march him to the cells. The prisoner is going back to prison, so it seems pretty obvious that he won't be free for a while, but Rothbard's definition entails that no one's freedom is compromised here because nobody's rights are violated. Or, some person, A, steals your precious object, x. Later, you confront A and threaten to shoot A dead unless A returns x. A complies with your threat. Here, you have obviously coerced A – he doesn't return the x of his own free will – but, according to Rothbard's definition this couldn't even happen because A had no right to the object in the first place. On the other hand, there can be cases where your rights *are* violated but *not* your liberty. For example, suppose that your

next door neighbour's small child sneaks through the fence into your
garden, retrieves his lost ball, and then returns to his own garden. The
child has invaded your property, and so 'violated' a right of yours. Has he
coerced you or subjected you to his will? Has he – even – turned you into
a slave? Has he, perhaps, committed an act of aggression against you?
Obviously not. If you hadn't been looking out of the window at the time
you wouldn't even have noticed. (Incidentally, we should note that aggression differs from coercion in that it is not, *conceptually* speaking an 'opposite'
of freedom at all. Acts of aggression can – contingently – result in a loss of
freedom sometimes, but the two are not definitionally tied.)

So, just as libertarians try to persuade us to revise our morality, to re-define
it in terms of the 'rights-fence' model, so they re-define 'freedom' in terms of
the same model. It is instructive to pause here to consider what this amounts
to. If the ideal world, where everyone keeps to his or her side of the fence, is
equivalent to the moral order, and if this is also the world where everyone
respects the freedom of all the others, then we are confronted with something
rather old-fashioned; a grandiose metaphysical system according to which the
All is the One – The Realm of Rights, The Ultimate Moral Order, and the
Realm of True Freedom being all three equivalent.

The balloon is easily pricked with the help of a few ordinary and
down-to-earth examples (the prisoner, the thief, the child); and the fact
leads me, at least, to reflect that the incident to which Wittgenstein refers
in his letter (quoted at the opening of Part II) was one of those small events
which can be seen, in retrospect, to have contained in microcosm the
beginnings of something altogether more significant and tragic. Wittgenstein may well have considered it important for philosophers to get their
hands dirty, and it is on record that he held strong left-wing political
sympathies, at least for a while.[2] However, you'd never guess any of this
from reading the *Philosophical Investigations*. In common with the other
founding figures of 'ordinary language' analytic philosophy (Austin, Ryle),
Wittgenstein, in his more profound and technical writing, had little to say
on the subject of ethics and nothing at all on politics.[3] The result was that
political philosophy went out of fashion for a time. This led to the quite
mistaken impression that analytic philosophy is of no relevance to political
thought. At one time it was even identified – famously, by Peter Laslett –
as one of the culprits responsible for killing political philosophy off.[4] We
now see the result. Many on the Left – no doubt suspecting this emphasis
on 'ordinary usage' to have conservative implications – have preferred to
vacate the field and, instead, to pursue exotic Derridean cul-de-sacs. This
has left it wide open for the Right to occupy; seizing, as it were, the many
photo-opportunities available for posing amongst formidable ghosts.

But although we see reactionary theory assuming the analytic mantle stylistically, as in the case of libertarianism, it does so in few other respects; and the 'later' Wittgenstein's epitaph for his 'earlier' ideas will also serve very well to mark libertarianism's final resting place: 'A picture held us captive' (Wittgenstein 1953: 48).

2   THE REALM OF RIGHTS AND THE ECONOMIC OR-DER

We should also consider the relation between rights-based libertarianism and economic theory, not only because libertarianism attaches central importance to an economic institution, the market, but because the former, when it isn't sounding like philosophy, draws quite heavily upon the technical jargon of the latter. Indeed, some more consequentialist libertarians – Friedman and Hayek are the most obvious examples – tend to be thought of as economists rather than philosophers. (And if they have acquired more status as a result, perhaps this is characteristic of our times too.)

Moreover, it is easy to see how libertarianism could come to be mistakenly perceived as an economic theory, because – at a superficial level – some tenets of both are almost indistinguishable. We have already noted this feature while considering the reducibility (or 'nothing more than') thesis. This turned out on examination to be an ethical claim, despite its superficial resemblance to the (no doubt sound) methodological principle that laws of economics are the result, or outcome, of multiple bilateral exchanges. Just to give another example, the libertarian thesis according to which both the bilateral exchange and, via reducibility, the market system as a whole are paradigmatic of mutual beneficiality is reminiscent both of Say's (classical) Law according to which, in principle, the economy will always absorb the commodities it is capable of producing, and of the ('neo-classical', 'monetarist') tenet that 'a modern industrial economy, if left to itself, is self-stabilising at full employment' (Stewart 1986: 43, 158).[5]

However, these superficial appearances can mask the following fundamental difference *of aim* between economic theory on the one hand and libertarian philosophy on the other. Economic theory aims to be value-neutral; to unravel the workings of an economy with a view to achieving ends which are themselves external to the theory. It is in this way that, armed with a good theory, the economist puts himself or herself into a position to say to the administrator, for example, 'If you want to cut inflation, you must do such-and-such, but if you want to create employment you must do such-and-such.' (Whether economic theory ever achieves value-neutrality is quite another question of course, but that is its aim nevertheless.) In sharp contrast, libertarian philosophy is anything but value-neutral. It says that, whatever else you do, you must make sure that people's rights are respected. Anything else – reducing inflation, creating employment, 'growth' – must take second place because you must never, on any account, allow a pattern to upset liberty.

For many of their readers, the full import of this view is probably masked by the fact that rights-based libertarians tend to assume the truth of the invisible hand thesis. Or else, they are likely to agree with Nozick's statement of faith: 'I believe that the free operation of a market system will not actually run afoul of the Lockean proviso' (1974: 182). (According to 'the Lockean proviso' a person who expropriates from the common stock acquires a right only if that person ensures that 'enough and as good' is left over for others. If Nozick is right, the repetition of 'productive exchanges' characteristic of a market economy will not – or not normally – leave third parties worse off.)[6] Now, a world in which the market actually worked to ensure the maximum possible satisfaction of wants might be quite tolerable, even for those who are not especially attached to the libertarian account of rights. But what if the invisible hand thesis is false? After all, there can be many types of hand, and what if, not Smith's, but some other equally blind but more malign hand is at work behind the scenes? Suppose, for example, that Keynes rather than Smith is right. If Keynes is right, the free operation of an economy left to itself can stabilise at a level below full employment. In other words, it can lead to massive economic depression and high levels of unemployment (Keynes 1973). The libertarian must sanction this situation provided that it has arisen from a process which violates no one's libertarian entitlements, as it will be the case where the 'pure' free market is at work. The sub-maximal equilibrium will be just one more pattern, and libertarianism cannot allow interference with liberty in order to establish a different pattern.

Three points arise from this. The first is that even if nothing else were sufficient to establish libertarianism's complete moral bankruptcy, its commitment to this conclusion would be. After disease and premature death, sustained unemployment is one of the worst evils which can befall an ordinary person. In the modern world, the unemployed person loses more than money. That person loses the ability to plan ahead and to organise his or her life. This can amount to losing the ability to give that life a coherent meaning. It is very likely that he or she will lose a sense of identity, dignity and self-respect as well. A pure free market system can deprive a person of these things at a stroke, callously. So, it seems that libertarianism is logically committed to viciously contravening the very values upon which it purports to be premised; Kantian respect for the innate worth and separateness of persons.

Second, and related to the first point, it is possible to question the *force* of the 'rights-fence' model. One only has to ask oneself what it would be like to be an unemployed person in a sustained period of economic depression.[7] In this situation, even if people do have libertarian entitlements, *why should it matter* that they do? If remedial measures, in the form of public works financed by taxation, can be taken, *who could reasonably object* if a few 'rights-fences' have to be crossed in the process? Here, the violations involved are so obviously outweighed by the greater evil to be tackled that any reasonably minded libertarian must be forced to drop the claim that rights, and only rights, always count against the upsetting of patterns.

Third, the framework of libertarian doctrine is so constructed that the following otherwise evident fact falls right through the gaps in its structure: a person who is rendered or kept unemployed suffers a serious violation of his or her freedom. For one thing, poverty will erect obstacles to prevent that person doing things he or she could otherwise do. He or she will thus lack 'negative' freedom. Further, the unemployed person is – like the victim of coercion – 'subject to the will of another'; perhaps not so much to the original employer who can claim to have sacked the workforce as a response to market forces, but certainly, and more criminally, to the agents of government who could intervene but do not. Against this, libertarians will no doubt argue that 'facts of nature' do not render actions involuntary and so on, but it should be clear by now that any such response is completely inadequate.

3 THE LIBERTARIAN, THE SAMARITAN AND THE STATE

It only remains to consider how the 'rights-fence' model conditions the libertarian view of the state, which – as readers will have gathered – is not libertarianism's favourite institution. To avoid any misunderstanding, let me add that neither is it mine. The history of the modern nation-state, at least, is far too hypocritically mendacious and bloodstained to inspire much genuine affection.

Libertarians tend to define the state with the help of two minimally necessary conditions. According to the first, to qualify as a state any 'agency' must exercise the monopoly of coercive force over a given geographical area. The second states that the coercive agency must claim legitimacy; that is, the right to exercise coercive force.[8] This seems reasonable enough to me. At any rate, it certainly captures the way in which modern nation-states tend to perceive themselves, although I should add that I am unsure how the first condition is affected by the fact that, in reality, citizens of modern states are also prey to the coercive force exercised by, for example, the huge capitalist corporations which operate across their territory. Does this falsify the definition by showing that states can exist where the first condition doesn't hold, or should we say that – since the corporations only operate with the state's permission – the definition remains intact? And what if an attempt to withdraw that permission were to result in the collapse, not of the corporations, but of the state? (None of this would worry libertarians, who redefine 'coercion' to preclude the possibility of capitalism being coercive. But I am unconvinced by that type of argument so it worries me.)

Still, determining the *precise* nature of the state is a problem we needn't pursue, because the question at issue relates only to the undeniable fact that states exercise coercion. The 'rights-fence' model puts an absolute prohibition on coercion, which it defines in terms of 'boundary-crossings' and, given this, it is clear that where libertarians accept the need for a state at all they can only do so grudgingly. As one might expect, some libertarians – Rothbard is the most well-known example – are out-and-out anarchists. Others, less optimistic about the possibility of people's rights being rendered secure where there is no state whatsoever, advocate a state, though no more than a 'minimal' state whose function is limited to protecting rights. (The main disagreement between Rothbard and Nozick, for example, is over how the law will be defined and enforced in a world run according to libertarian principles. Rothbard thinks that this can be done by private law enforcement agencies, whereas Nozick sets out an ingenious account of how, from a State of Nature, persons forming such agencies will 'back into a state without really trying' (1974: Part I).

But 'rights as fences' is an inaccurate and distorted metaphor for the moral universe and, in particular, it overstates the absoluteness of the prohibition against coercion. Libertarianism's attitude to the state rests upon the metaphor and is likely to be equally distorted. Are there not acceptable ways of justifying the state – or, if not the state, then at least some form of coercive public agency – which the metaphor mistakenly precludes? I have argued for the metaphor's inadequacy by contrasting it with the Good Samaritan story so, to begin with, let us note that the latter is *also* an inadequate model for the state. If we are to turn the metaphor into a good analogy for the latter we need to vary it in a way which makes it plausible to add two features. First, we need to introduce a third party and imagine a situation in which an otherwise unwilling Samaritan is *forced* to aid the victim by someone else. (This could be a second Samaritan –

call him 'Samaritan 2'.) Second, we need an explanation of why Samaritan 2 has the *authority* to force Samaritan 1 to help. If I see you committing a crime, I do not have the authority to punish you. Only the state has. We need an analogy for this feature of real states.

However, these features are reflected in many arguments for the state. They are common and familiar arguments no doubt, but none the worse for that. Thus, so far as the first feature is concerned, we need only entertain the possibility of there being actions which need to be taken – where, maybe, it is morally required that they should be taken – but where they can only be taken if others are compelled to act in concert by a public agency. Law enforcement may be one good example, as Nozick half-concedes.[9] Others are as follows. It may be that some public utility upon which everyone relies (water, electricity, a railway) would fail if it were run privately and that the state must step in, financing the operation of the utility through taxation. Even Smith would agree with this.[10] Or it may be that the poor and starving can be numbered in millions; that there are, as it were, many millions of victims in the ditch. A single individual's attempt to help will be ineffective. Maybe that individual will see no point in even trying unless he or she can be sure that others, more reluctant, are being constrained to assist. Or the economy, left to itself, will eventually collapse for good Keynesian reasons. Only some forward planning and intervention by a central agency will save things. Such everyday scenarios will only look unconvincing to those religiously overimpressed by the myth of the invisible hand. And so far as the second feature, authority, is concerned, autonomous (twentieth/twenty-first-century) persons who wish to take responsibility for their own lives will want state actions ratified democratically.

Such familiar arguments raise familiar further questions, of course. Exactly where is one to draw the line between morally justifiable state intervention and morally objectionable, nosey-parker, state interference? How convincing is it – really – to describe our own antique constitutional structures as 'democratic' in the sense that they genuinely facilitate self-determination for autonomous beings? But the point is that these are genuine questions and serious attempts to answer them need to be made. Libertarianism's central metaphor artificially forecloses any intelligent attempt to deal with them. Let me say that I, for one, am unimpressed by libertarian arguments to the effect that, since the former line is difficult to draw, it must follow that it does not exist.[11] And, while there may be some inevitable artificiality in representing democratic institutions of any sort as fully enabling self-government, that is nowhere near so artificial as the libertarian pretence that a free market does better in this respect.

There is another distortion too, one which is common to *both* the 'rights-fence' metaphor *and* the Samaritan story. In my earlier argument, the latter provided a good contrast for the former mainly because I was focusing upon Nozick's attempt to undermine the case for the welfare state. In effect, the libertarian is asking why the victim (or anyone) should get a 'welfare handout' and can come up with no answer. Against this, the parable portrays a situation in which there is an overwhelming moral case for 'welfare handouts' (if only to those who have just been beaten up and left for dead). However, this response to libertarianism will only appear fully adequate to those who are satisfied with a state whose function is merely ameliorative; that is, which acts as a charitable organisation for helping those who would otherwise suffer the worst, but does nothing more.

Well, perhaps there are those who are satisfied by this and perhaps the fact has been of some historical significance. The very phrase, 'welfare state', seems to embody this limited ideal, and one wonders whether it can be just an accident that, even in the relatively prosperous 1960s, the proportion of adult UK citizens 'in poverty' was much the same as it had been before 1914 (Thane 1982: 288). The conjecture becomes all the more depressing when one considers that even a welfare state does more than redistribute wealth in order to alleviate poverty. In education, for example, a view which treats the state provision of schooling as a 'handout' to those who cannot afford to pay for the private education of their children will never do full justice to the role an education system can and should play in changing the world for the better.[12]

In conclusion, here is how I see it: autonomous human beings who aspire to self-determination will require institutions which are in certain respects coercive if they are to shape their world in ways they consider desirable. They will seek to influence *all* aspects of that world in accordance with *a whole range* of values. The ameliorative 'welfare state' model fails to recognise this. Libertarianism feeds off this model by spending too much time attacking it. Who knows what structures the global village we increasingly inhabit will eventually throw up?

Part III

They spent New Year's Day in that house, a New Year's Day apparently remembered by Dickens forty-six years later in an article for his journal, *Household Words*. 'So far back do my recollections of childhood extend', he wrote, 'that I have a vivid remembrance of the sensation of being carried down-stairs in a woman's arms, and holding tight to her, in the terror of seeing the steep perspective below'. This has the ring of truthful memory, a recollected experience of anxiety, and so does the picture which greeted him when he peeped into the celebrations in the ground floor room – '. . . a very long row of ladies and gentlemen sitting against a wall, all drinking at once out of little glass cups with handles, like custard-cups. . . . There was no speech making, no quick movement and change of action, no demonstration of any kind. They were all sitting in a long row against the wall – very like my first idea of the good people in Heaven, as I derived it from a wretched picture in a Prayer-book – and they had all got their heads a little thrown back, and were drinking all at once.' This is an extraordinary picture; it was one that he said always haunted him when anyone talked of a New Year's Day party. But in this vision of a row of strangely silent people, leaning against a wall with their heads thrown back, there also is revived the picture of a lost age, a vanished age – lost to Charles Dickens himself when he looks back, but also how much lost to us.

Peter Ackroyd, Dickens

Chapter 10

The good fairy's wand

The claim that wide-eyed trust in the free market has more in common with fundamentalist religious faith than it does with any philosophically well-founded and defensible position is becoming increasingly a common-place. People you meet – at dinner parties and suchlike social occasions – will frequently tell you as much (unless they are trying to persuade you of the reverse, that is). One of my aims has been to bear the commonplace out by demonstrating, through an analysis of the best arguments for the free market I can think of, that it states a truth. Now, because this study would be incomplete without an examination of less rights-based, more consequentialist, forms of libertarianism, we must turn to some of the worst. It is generally known that there is such a thing as the invisible hand argument, but far less widely realised just how bad – how thin and tawdry – so many versions of that argument are. These, the more usual forms of invisible handism, form the subject of this chapter.

1 VULGAR INVISIBLE-HANDISM

The reader will recall that 'vulgar invisible-handism', as I shall call it from now, presupposes a distinction between private, or 'self', interest on the one hand and, on the other, the general interest or public good. It states that the unrestricted pursuit of the former (unrestricted except by laws which defend private property and freedom of contract, of course) leads, unintentionally and 'as if by an invisible hand', to the realisation of the latter. In other words, it states that 'private vice is public virtue'. Still, 'vice' and 'virtue' are not especially helpful terms here, and neither are 'self-interest' or 'public good', so, to be as fair to the argument as possible, we should respecify it.

Proponents of invisible-handism may or may not have especially self-centred or selfish motives in mind (Mandeville obviously did, others may not), but the point of the claim is clear either way. We should take 'self-interest' to mean – simply – that sort of interest which can be satisfied by the free market left to itself. This might not be 'selfish' in the ordinary sense. For example, someone who rushes to the pharmacist's late at night to purchase medicine for a tiresome, but sick, relative is acting 'unselfishly' in the ordinary sense of that phrase, but, nevertheless, this person can be said to have an 'interest' for which the market successfully caters. We must also respecify 'the general interest' because most proponents of the thesis, in common with libertarians generally, tend to insist that 'society' is 'nothing more than the sum of the individuals who compose it' and not, for example, some supra-personal entity or 'body politic' with a will and an interest of its own. Therefore, we must construe the phrase to mean that state of affairs in which each individual's interest is satisfied to the greatest degree possible. What state of affairs is that? Libertarians and invisible-handers are not well disposed towards equality, so I suggest that we take it to be that state of affairs in which, although it may contain inequalities, those worst off (as well as everyone else, or at least most people) are better off than they would be under any other alternative arrangement. (The situation would roughly align with Rawls's 'difference principle'.)

Thus respecified in the interests of fairness and accuracy, the invisible hand claim reads as follows:

The Invisible Hand Thesis: It is invariably (or almost invariably) the case that, where individuals are left to pursue their own aims in their own way under free market conditions, the result is that everyone (or almost everyone), including the worst off, is rendered better off than he or she would be under any other conditions.

The phrase which causes trouble here is – of course – 'invariably (or almost invariably)'. However, this has to be included. Few libertarians would go so far as to exalt the thesis to the status of a necessary truth, or insist that it must always hold in every conceivable circumstance; but unless we take the claim to be that the number of exceptions to the otherwise iron rule is so small that it is practically negligible, we don't have an invisible hand thesis at all – just the modest and reasonable assertion that it is sometimes better to leave things to the market. With the inclusion of the 'near invariability' assumption, though, the thesis is left wide open to some apparently plain and obvious objections.

For example, first, there is one way in which the thesis appears to contradict obvious logical sense. Its libertarian proponents are opposed to 'welfarist' governmental measures involving the taxation of the relatively rich to finance the poor and relatively poor. Governments predisposed to invisible-handism will therefore reduce the tax 'burden' on the former and, which comes to the same thing, cut aid in the form of benefits and so on to the latter. This looks a lot like making the poor *poorer*. But, according to the invisible hand story, the market renders the worst off better off than they would otherwise be. It seems reasonable to ask: how can it be claimed without a ridiculously self-evident contradiction that *by making people worse off one makes them better off at the same time?*

Second, there are a number of factual considerations which present a strong *prima facie* case against the thesis. I have already outlined this (see pp. 30–1). So, third, let me now add to it that the world as a whole is faced with a number of serious crises to which it is – as a matter of fact – not at all obvious that the market provides a solution. This becomes particularly apparent in cases where the state, as the agency responsible for directing economic policy within some given geographical area, falls to the edge of the picture because international action appears to be demanded. Examples are:

1   Aids: The World Health Organisation has recently estimated that an *eightfold* increase in expenditure is needed if we are to have a hope of tackling the Aids crisis. What are we supposed to do, wait until some benevolent trillionaire comes up with the money? (Does anyone have that much money?) Certainly the majority of those presently affected – being African and Asian peasants – are unlikely to pay for research, care and education out of their own personal fortunes.

2   War: There seems to be no better reason for thinking that capitalism must bring wars to a halt than for thinking of war as capitalism's inevitable result. Isn't war, at least sometimes, just 'competition by other means'? And, within the libertarian Utopia, what will substitute for the United Nations, which is, after all, a forum for representatives of *states?* Will anything substitute for it?

3   Pollution: In its most problematic forms this also crosses national boundaries. Isn't it reasonable to suppose that the market left to itself will not, or not very often, supply capitalists, primarily concerned to increase profits, with a sufficient incentive to take anti-pollution measures?

So here are examples of difficulties to which libertarianism tends to pay too little attention, thanks to the way it focuses too closely on, and so in a way feeds off, its favourite bogey, the 'state as coercive agency with a monopoly of power within a given geographical area'.

Fourth, there is the historical record to consider. The invisible hand thesis appears to stand in contradiction to the evident fact that this century's two most systematic attempts to impose monetary discipline in line with classical, and then neo-classical, economic theory (to both of which invisible-handism is central) have been followed by devastating depressions. I mean the return to the gold standard in the 1920s and the imposition of Reaganite/Thatcherite economic policies throughout a large part of the West in the 1980s. Not that the evidence counts conclusively against the thesis. Its proponents can argue that the economic measures taken just didn't go far enough (some do),[1] but only the converted and born-again will fail to suspect a causal connection here.

2 THE GOOD FAIRY'S WAND

In fact, there is nothing conclusive about anything contained in the preceding paragraphs. All I have done is raise questions, although I think they are questions which more sceptical and level-headed readers will feel inclined to answer in ways which run counter to invisible-handism. But this simply presents a challenge to which libertarian proponents of the thesis must respond. This they tend to do in at least one of three ways. Let us call these arguments 1, 2 and 3.

2.1 Argument 1

This rules those 'interests' which cannot be satisfied by the market out of account as unworthy of consideration. Exactly how depends on the version. Perhaps it will be claimed that they are not 'real' or 'genuine' interests, or perhaps some other reason will be found for not taking them seriously. We have already encountered this manoeuvre in the way Sir Keith Joseph condescendingly discounts the interests of his unworldly and otherwise unbourgeois 'saints and ascetics' (Joseph and Sumption 1979: 119). One source of its appeal for libertarians is that it helps 'save' the reducibility thesis by defining counter-examples to it out of existence. But, in any case, the move fails because it is just not the case that all interests which cannot be satisfied by the market must be unworldly or even unself-interested. It is pretty obviously self-interested (in a perfectly ordinary sense of 'self-interested') to desire that the air one breathes should be clean and unpolluted, for example, and, if the market cannot satisfy it, this interest cannot be dismissed as spurious.

2.2 Argument 2

By contrast with the first, argument 2 takes interests as it finds them and does not rest upon an arbitrary redefinition of the term 'interest'. The argument states – just as one might expect it to – that there are more to things than might initially appear from first impressions or surface appearances. According to argument 2, the free market is *really* working to satisfy all types of interest all the time, even when it isn't obvious. This – the most common libertarian move – fails for a number of reasons, the first being that it tends to assume the existence of certain background conditions. As so often, Rothbard is a good source of illustration. Take the following massively over-optimistic scenario:

> [C]onsider what would happen if private firms were able to own the rivers and the lakes. If a private firm owned Lake Erie, for example, then anyone dumping garbage in the lake would be promptly sued in the courts for their aggression against private property and would be forced by the courts to pay damages and to cease and desist from any further aggression. Thus, only private property rights will insure an end to pollution-invasion of resources. Only because rivers are unowned is there no owner to rise up and defend his precious resource from attack.
>
> (1973: 255)

If Rothbard is right, the solution to the environmental crisis is simple and easily within reach. But is he right? One question I raised earlier was whether the market can (almost invariably) be relied upon to supply capitalists with a sufficient motive to pay for expensive anti-pollution measures, so let us ask *why* the private owner of Lake Erie should be so interested in keeping it clean. Why not assume, alternatively, that the private company concerned has decided that it can generate the most wealth for itself by allowing another large company, at a price, to use the lake as a dump for nuclear waste? The scenario is no less plausible than Rothbard's and it demonstrates that Rothbard is simply assuming the presence of a condition which may not exist; in this case a desire on the part of the owner to keep the water pure. Rothbard's assumption parallels Adam Smith's, that market agents would necessarily prefer 'the support of domestic to that of foreign industry' (1976: 477–8). *Why* would they? Smith's assumption may have been natural enough in the late eighteenth century, but, these days, why not equally assume that people would prefer cheap foreign imports? So, the argument fails because the invisible hand thesis is supposed to show that the market *guarantees* the public good, not just in certain circumstances but in almost all.

Note that the libertarian cannot convincingly reply to this by insisting that, if the lake were used as a nuclear dump, those living around its shores – being themselves owners, if only of their 'persons' – would inevitably rise up and defend their interests against the company's aggression. A second reason for the failure of this argument is that it tends to equate *having a motive* to perform an action with *being motivated to act*. But the two are not equivalent, because whereas the former does not necessarily culminate in a person's acting (or at least trying to act) the latter does. For example, every heavy smoker aware of the risks has a motive for giving up – a very strong one – but everyone who continues to smoke despite this is quite evidently not motivated to give up. Similarly, while there can be no doubt that a free market framework supplies every individual with motives for acting in certain ways and not others – it attaches 'costs' and 'benefits' to alternative courses of action – it doesn't follow that they will act in those ways. For example, what if Lake Erie has become so polluted by the nuclear waste that the only people who live around its shores are slum-dwellers who can find nowhere better to live? What if they rent their homes from landlords who have chosen to live elsewhere on the proceeds, in safer surroundings? What if the shore-dwellers are unable to afford legal representation (as they might be if the lawyers are all busily employed defending the landlords, so that there is no one to step into this particular market niche)? What if the landlords work as executives for the company owning the lake, and what if the shore-dwellers consequently fear eviction? Provided that one assumes a pure free market, there is nothing especially fantastic or improbable about any of this. Who can forecast patterns? The shore-dwellers still have a very good motive for suing the owners, but *will* they? Will they *really*?

Individuals act from many types of motive, of course, and not just those deriving from the way the market sets things up for them (the costs and benefits). Suppose, to take yet another scenario, that the owner of Lake Erie is an incredibly rich absentee landlord. This person – there are plenty of real examples in history – has a strong economic motive for either exploiting the lake's potential or just selling it. But what if he or she chooses, for whatever reason, not to bother? What if that is why the garbage gets in there? A further reason for the failure of argument 2 is that it tends to forget that one cannot exclude such 'non-economic' motives and, at the same time, tell a credible story. Here is nineteenth century history according to Rothbard.

[F]actory smoke and many of its bad effects have been known ever since the Industrial Revolution, known to the extent that the American courts, during the late – and as far back as the early – nineteenth century made the deliberate decision to allow property rights to be violated by industrial smoke. To do so, the courts had to – and did – systematically change and weaken the defences of property rights embedded in Anglo-Saxon common law ... during the nineteenth century, the courts systematically altered the law of negligence and the law of nuisance to *permit* any air pollution which was not unusually greater than any similar manufacturing firm, one that was not more extensive than the customary practice of polluters.

(1973: 257) (emphasis in original)

In this remarkably – wonderfully – self-contradictory passage we are invited to draw the conclusion that private property *must* provide the solution to the pollution problem from an account of how it clearly did *not*. If the nineteenth century witnessed a move from an initial situation of well-defended property rights to a later situation in which great pollution was tolerated, as Rothbard claims, *it cannot have provided this solution*. I think it likely that Rothbard would reply to this that the system wasn't 'pure' enough and so sinister interests came into play. On such an account, the courts would have been motivated to act as they did by pressure from government, which would have been, in turn, motivated to act as it did by pressure from powerful industrialists. But how pure does the system have to be if it is to contain the sinister interests? (Rothbard can't just ignore their existence. It could be that he is trying to do exactly that.) Can it be purified further by removing the government from the story, as Rothbard would, no doubt, like? The trouble is that we need a reason for believing that the motives would then be contained, whereas there is far more reason for thinking that, in reality, the powerful industrialists would then have exerted just the same pressure, if not more, on privately-owned courts.

In summary, then, argument 2 – the characteristically libertarian argument according to which if some item, x, were privately owned then a truly wonderful event, y, would almost certainly happen – deserves the comment that maybe it would, but even then, and still only maybe, only in Valhalla.

2.3 Argument 3

As for argument 3, this is really a variant of the previous one, but one which manages to absolve itself of any reference to the ascertainable whatsoever. According to argument 3, interference with the market has detrimental effects, if not here and now, then for others living far away or else for our descendants in the distant future. Even Hayek, who really should have known better, is guilty of this one. He writes, for example, that 'morals are concerned with effects in the long run – effects *beyond our possible perception*' (Hayek 1988: 57) (emphasis in original). This clearly raises the question of why this alleged fact should count as a guide to our actions now, and of how much it should count if it counts at all. Imagine saying to a Neanderthal, 'Instead of waiting for extinction, why don't you do us all a favour and commit suicide now. That way, *homo sapiens*, with his inspiring market order, will have a chance to evolve earlier.' It also merits the comment that it is at least immune to disproof. As with the fairies at the bottom of the garden, the ones who are so shy that they hide away whenever a human approaches, the non-existence of those unfortunate future others who will suffer from our present 'constructivist rationalist' meddling can never be conclusively demonstrated.

It is in a way surprising that Hayek should advance such a naive argument, because his main thesis – the thesis of 'spontaneous order' – is altogether superior to the arguments I have just considered, and immune to at least some of the objections I have raised. It is the most subtle, interesting and credible version of the invisible hand argument there is. That is why the next chapter is devoted to it. If there are reasons for rejecting Hayek's argument, there is little point in considering others further. I should add that Hayek himself does not especially like the term 'invisible hand' and prefers, for example, 'unsurveyable pattern' (1988: 14). Nevertheless, I think the characterisation fair enough. Hayek should bear in mind that, where a usage has a long and settled history, as in this case, there is some good reason for sticking to it, even if it is a usage one doesn't like much. Had it been up to me, I would have labelled the argument – at least in its more vulgar variants – 'the tale of the good fairy's magic wand'.

Chapter 11

Hayek and the hand of fate

In 1944 George Orwell reviewed Hayek's *The Road to Serfdom* for the *Observer* in the following terms:

> Capitalism leads to dole queues, the scramble for markets, and war. Collectivism leads to concentration camps, leader worship, and war. There is no way out of this unless a planned economy can be somehow combined with the freedom of the intellect, which can only happen if the concept of right and wrong is restored to politics.
>
> (Orwell 1968: 144)

Hayek's last book, *The Fatal Conceit*, appeared as recently as 1988, and in it Hayek continued to pursue and elaborate upon the themes of his earlier work. In fact, Hayek's central concerns and positions remained remarkably constant throughout his long and productive life. Similar arguments invite correspondingly similar criticisms, so it won't come as too much of a surprise to find this reflected in the fact that the conclusion I shall draw here resembles Orwell's. However, that conclusion will (I think) be less pessimistically over-stated and (if anything) yet more tentatively pragmatic. Unlike Orwell – and unlike Hayek – I can see no good reason for thinking that one thing must in due course lead to another, or that, for a great many things, those things won't lead to something quite different. There is no secret formula, and in the real world there is – I am afraid – no substitute for the piecemeal application of clumsy human intelligence to the specific situation.

The right place to begin is with an outline of Hayek's thesis and a summary of its considerable merits.

1 THE MARKET AS A SPONTANEOUS ORDER

1.1 Hayek's thesis

Central to Hayek's thesis is the idea that the market is a 'spontaneous order', the result of human action but not of deliberate design and, in that sense, the delicately balanced outcome of an evolutionary process. An 'order' is defined by Hayek as 'a state of affairs in which a multiplicity of elements are so related to each other that we may learn from our acquaintance with some spatial or temporal part of the whole to form correct expectations concerning the rest, or at least expectations which have a good chance of proving correct' (1982: 36). A 'spontaneous' order (or 'catallaxy') is a 'self-organising or self-generating system' or 'pattern'. It has not been deliberately designed or arranged, and we go wrong if we consider it 'due to the design of some thinking mind' (1982: 37, 36). Amongst the examples of spontaneous orders cited by Hayek are crystals and organic compounds, which 'we can never produce . . . by placing the individual atoms in such a position that they will form the lattice . . . or the system'. We can only 'create the conditions in which they will arrange themselves in such a manner' (1982: 40). A biological organism is also a spontaneous order (ibid.: 52).[1] The generation of a spontaneous order is, of course, contingent upon its constituent elements acting in certain regular ways. As Hayek says of the crystal, 'the regularity of the conduct of the elements will determine the general character of the resulting order but not all the detail of its particular manifestation' (ibid.: 40). Likewise, in biology, evolution is governed chemically, by 'rules' determining genetic expression, mutation and so on, although the 'particular manifestation' – the specific characteristics of the organism which eventually evolves – will also result from the interaction of these with the environment to which that organism must adapt. By contrast, in the case of social 'orders' – morality, law, the market – the rules are learnt. 'The structure of social life is determined by rules of conduct which manifest themselves only by being in fact observed' (ibid.: 43). Their evolution proceeds culturally, not genetically, which is not to deny that there are, nevertheless, in a very good sense of 'natural', undoubtedly 'natural' phenomena (ibid.: 20ff).

In Hayek's view, the market's great virtues are twofold. There is, first and most significantly, a functional virtue to consider. Hayek holds that the naturally or 'spontaneously' evolved market is the best allocative device we have, the reason being that only the market can accommodate the inescapable fact of human *ignorance*. 'A designer or engineer needs all the data and full power to control or manipulate them if he is to organise the material objects to produce the intended result' (1982: 12), but no single person could possibly possess all the information necessary to organise and guide behaviour in the way the market does. Competition is held to compensate for this by serving as a 'discovery procedure'. Within a free market, prices convey 'information in coded form' and so give 'anyone who has the opportunity to exploit special circumstances the possibility to do so profitably' as well as 'by conveying to the other parties that there is some such opportunity' (ibid.: 117). Efficiency – even the improvement in 'the relative position of those in the lowest income groups' resulting from the 'general growth of wealth' (ibid.: 131) – is facilitated by the fact that prices indicate 'which of the available technical methods is the most economical in the given circumstances' (ibid.: 117). Moreover – and most importantly for Hayek – this is achieved without presupposing that participants within the market 'game' share common ends or values, and without imposing any such system of common ends upon them. It is in these respects that the spontaneous market order crucially differs from any artificial or 'made' order. The latter is deliberately constructed for a particular purpose and, whereas 'a spontaneous order may extend to circumstances so complex that no mind can comprehend them all' (ibid.: 41) (because we only need 'acquaintance with some spatial or temporal part of the whole to form correct expectations concerning the rest'), this is not the case for an artificial order. To suppose otherwise is to commit what Hayek calls the fallacy of 'constructivist rationalism'. According to Hayek, all forms of socialism are guilty of this and *The Fatal Conceit* is thus subtitled *The Errors of Socialism*.

On Hayek's account, the market's other great virtue is, in a word, survival. The concept is variously glossed by Hayek, but his main point is that the cultural traditions embodied within liberalism (as Hayek conceives it) and the market order have won the evolutionary competition against other, more 'closed' and 'tribal', arrangements (see Hayek 1988: 16). It is certainly his view that the relative 'success' of Western civilisation is closely connected with respect for 'open' traditions. Of this, he writes that 'We can preserve an order of such complexity . . . only indirectly by enforcing and improving the rules conducive to the formation of a spontaneous order' (1982: 51). Elsewhere, Hayek overstates his case with improbable claims such as 'The dispute between the market order and socialism is no less than a matter of survival' (1988: 7) and he occasionally equates cultural survival with population increase; a highly dubious manoeuvre. But the main claim – the first – is clear enough, even though there seems to be no obvious and precise lesson to be drawn from it. If Hayek's description of the market order is right, then, having stood the test of evolutionary time, that order must be no mean animal and should be treated with respect; but then the dinosaur stood the same test, at least for a time, and that was an awesome beast too. And, of course, there would be no great virtue in the market's having survived unless its survival were the cause of our own, which is what Hayek thinks. As he says, 'although this morality is not "justified" by the fact that it enables us . . . to survive, *it does enable us to survive, and there is perhaps something to be said for that*' (1988: 70) (emphasis in the original).

1.2 The merits of Hayek's thesis

The best way to illuminate these is to contrast Hayek's account with other pro-free market positions. For example, it is superior to Nozick's because Hayek does not boast a paranormal ability to see invisible fences. In other words, he does not proceed from the foundationless assertion that there exists a mysterious realm of natural rights. In contrast to Nozick, Hayek is scornfully sceptical of the very idea that we just 'have' such rights in the way that we 'have' brains and opposable thumbs. He remarks, for example, that 'Mere existence cannot confer a right or moral claim on anyone against any other' (1988: 152). Moreover, and in line with this, Hayek does not indulge in blanket assertions concerning the scope of property. On the contrary, he is well aware that 'property' is a concept of a certain complexity and open to re-definition. Thus 'Because the drawing of boundaries serves a function . . . it is meaningful to ask whether in particular instances the boundary has been drawn in the right place, or whether in view of changed conditions an established rule is still adequate' (1982: 109). It is true enough that Hayek regards 'the delimitation of protected domains' – that is the institution of private property broadly construed to include 'property in the person', the rights to life, liberty and so on – as essential to the market's operation and consequently to human well being and survival. However, in Hayek's case, this claim is backed up by a subtle account of how and why the rules of conduct which define the domains develop. These rules determine 'only an abstract order which enables its members to derive from the particulars known to them expectations that have a good chance of being correct' (1982: 106).

In my view, the emphasis Hayek places on evolution is the strongest point in his favour, and not just because it provides a possible anchor for this thesis in scientifically well-established fact. Hayek claims – rightly, I think – that the notion of evolution was, in any case, originally borrowed by biology from the social sciences.[2] In fact, I would be surprised if *something like* Hayek's account of morality – of which his account of the market is a corollary – were not correct. For example, it gives a good explanation of *why* we have morality at all, and goes further than just pointing out that the moral attitude involves treating others as 'ends in themselves'. The fact requires explanation. It is certainly difficult – impossible in many cases – to supply the self-interested person (or group) with a rationale for always doing the right thing, especially when it is more obviously advantageous to do the reverse, and yet the rules continue to hold their force. An account along the lines of Hayek's, according to which rules evolve without our always being able to say why we follow them, could hold the key.

It is also noteworthy that Hayek manages to avoid many of the pitfalls to which vulgar invisible-handism is prone. For example, unlike others, Hayek does not seek to re-define 'interest' restrictively to include only that type of interest which can be satisfied by the market. Hayek's view is simply that the market creates 'conditions likely to improve the chances of all in the pursuit of their aims' whatever those 'mostly unknown' aims may be (1982: 2). Moreover, he doesn't need such redefinition to 'save' the reducibility thesis because his position does not commit him to reducibility. On the contrary, he holds – as I do – that the market exhibits features at the macro level which are indiscernible in its discrete 'micro' components. Nor does Hayek need to invent improbable fairy stories according to which everything works out to satisfy some public interest, definable as the sum of all private interests. Hayek is contemptuous of this type of notion and his view is, rather, that 'The order of the Great Society does rest and must rest on constant undesigned frustrations of some efforts – efforts which ought not to have been made but in free men can be discouraged only by failure' (1982: 2).

All this adds up to the following: if Hayek's theory were correct it would be nothing less than a version of the Fable of the Bees which, at the same time, recognises that we are not really bees at all and respects the essential separateness of persons. It would thus satisfy an important criterion. This looks promising.

2 HOW LIBERTARIAN IS HAYEK?

Although it is no doubt possible to call aspects of his 'evolutionism' into question, Hayek is certainly right to describe the market as a subtle device which is, in many circumstances, far superior to any deliberately designed substitute. (Remember that I am not out to criticise the market as such, but market *romances*; infatuated stories which imbue the market with inflated false significance.) However, it is consistent with this that the market should sometimes fail, and that such failure should need government intervention to rectify it. Hayek would agree. '*I am the last person to deny*', he writes, 'that increased wealth and the increased density of population have enlarged the number of collective needs which government can and should satisfy' (Hayek 1978: 111; emphasis mine); and '*Far from* advocating . . . a "minimal state", we find it unquestionable that in an advanced society government ought to use its power of raising funds by taxation to provide a number of services which for various reasons cannot be provided, or cannot be provided adequately, by the market' (1982: 41). Such strength of emphasis might easily lead the reader to wonder whether it can be right to count Hayek as a libertarian at all.

But he has more to say. Hayek's account of the market as a spontaneous order is interwoven with (Hayek would say it entails) a number of claims which are strongly in accordance with both the spirit and the letter of libertarianism more generally. For example, although Hayek thinks that government intervention is sometimes justified, his view is that, in reality, it is *hardly ever* justified, and then only when certain strict conditions are met. The core of his view is that the 'protection for private initiatives and enterprise' upon which the spontaneous order depends 'can only ever be achieved through the institution of private property and the whole aggregate of libertarian institutions of law' (1978: 190). Hayek's 'individual domains' are therefore *meant* to be more or less coterminous with private 'rights-territories' of the type presupposed by Nozick, even though each writer arrives at their existence via a different route. Hayek is almost always hostile to state and government and he is invariably, sometimes venomously, hostile to any form of socialism. So, in one way, it is no wonder that Hayek is a sort of guru for libertarians.

But now consider the following differences between Nozick and Hayek. As the reader will recall, Nozick limits justifiable state action to the minimum; protection against force, theft, fraud, and the enforcement of contracts. This means that a clear and definite line divides his position from that of 'the planner' who considers intervention justified for a whole range of purposes; 'welfare', progressive taxation to finance public services, overseas aid to the hungry, and so on. It is easy to see where Nozick stands, although, as we have seen, he pays the price for such decisiveness with an unsound metaphysic of the person. In contrast to Nozick, Hayek – like the planner – supports state intervention. If there is a difference between Hayek and the planner, it can only be a difference of 'less and more', that the former favours intervention far less often than the latter. So while Hayek's philosophy may rest on a more credible foundation than Nozick's, it pays a price in the form of a certain indeterminacy.

The question this raises is not, where does Hayek stand? It is, where *can* he stand? We know where he *wants* to stand – shoulder-to-shoulder with the libertarian right – but unless his 'spontaneous order' thesis can logically determine a stopping point or safety barrier, there is nothing to prevent him from sliding leftwards (logically, if not temperamentally) into a more reasonable and acceptable position. The stopping point exists only if it is true that the spontaneous order thesis logically entails the overtly libertarian moral prescriptions Hayek recommends.

3 SLIDES AND AMBIGUITIES

There is no such stopping point, and Hayek only manages to create the illusion of its existence with the help of some false inferences, slides and ambiguities. Let me now illustrate the point with a few examples.

3.1 Purpose and function

As a first, consider the role played by the close but distinct concepts of purpose and function within the context of Hayek's central distinction. We are told that 'the first important difference between a spontaneous order or *cosmos* and an organisation (arrangement) or *taxis* is that, not having been deliberately made by men, a *cosmos* has no purpose' (Hayek 1978: 73). This is clearly right. As the outcome of evolution, the market order can have no more purpose than the aggregate of natural species. It is, so to speak, 'simply there'. In contrast, the made order 'is necessarily designed for the achievement of particular ends or of a particular hierarchy of ends' (ibid.: 75). It is designed to achieve a purpose. Hayek stresses these points a great deal.

While the *cosmos* may be *purposeless*, however, it is not true to say that it has no *function*. And indeed, according to Hayek's account, there are many functions which it performs very well. Hayek mentions a number, and is sometimes quite specific, including not just 'survival' but, as noted previously, an increase in 'not only the absolute but also the relative position of those in the lowest income groups' and a raising of 'the income of the lowest groups more than the relatively higher ones' (1982: 131). (Rawls's difference principle again?)[3] So, while the spontaneous order has no purpose whereas the made order has, both the former and the latter can have a function. Indeed, it is conceivable that some given spontaneous order and some given made order might fulfil *exactly the same* function – enabling us to sustain more from discoverable resources, for example.

Consistent with this, Hayek's objection to 'planning' is not so much that it has a function but that, for the most part, it fulfils that function *badly*.

Why? Because – again for the most part – only the market can deploy 'knowledge dispersed among and accessible only to thousands or millions of separate individuals' (1978: 76). The qualification 'for the most part' is important here because there are, as noted, those cases where 'a number of services which for various reasons cannot be provided, or cannot be provided adequately, by the market' (1982: 41). Hayek's message is thus: don't mess around with things when, for all you know, you'll only make them worse. Only interfere when you can be reasonably confident of improving things.

It seems pretty obvious that this is no advice at all. Even if 'spontaneous order' is a good general description of the way the market usually tends to work, as a source of advice on how to act in specific cases it is useless. This bears out my conclusion (and Orwell's) that there is no magic formula, and it also raises the question of *how extensive* that class of things with which one shouldn't mess around is. So, here is the point. Unless it coincides more or less exactly with the class of things with which libertarians generally think one shouldn't mess around, the spontaneous order thesis provides no logical foundation for Hayek's libertarian ethic.

But there are plenty of reasons for thinking that the two classes are not at all co-extensive, because the number and magnitude of the problems which quite clearly do demand collective action and planned intervention is much greater than Hayek suggests. (Aids, war and pollution are examples.) If so, it follows – as I have been claiming – that the (plausible) spontaneous order thesis provides no logical support whatsoever for Hayek's (questionable) libertarian recommendations. Hayek would like it to. Like Rothbard, he would like us to resign ourselves to the hand of fate, to believe that all will be well if only we let the market take control. But, in fact, his evolutionism will not permit this.

Finally, note that this conclusion applies even within technical economic theory, Hayek's home territory. As an advocate of monetary control, Hayek holds that 'The cause of unemployment . . . is a deviation of prices and wages from their equilibrium position which would establish itself with a free market and monetary control' (Hayek 1978: 201). To this, the Keynesian (or neo-Keynesian) will reply that there are many equilibria and that 'A cut in real wages is . . . likely to reduce workers' consumption and, via the Multiplier mechanism . . . the incomes and consumption of other workers. Thus there will be a fall in the output of the economy and a rise, not a fall, in unemployment' (Stewart 1986: 184). But – whoever is right here – these are arguments over precisely how the market mechanism functions in a given situation. They are neither entailed nor contradicted by the spontaneous order thesis. They are simply independent of it. The thesis is more general in scope and paints a broad picture of how the market came about and of how – for the most part – it tends to function. It seems that one can even be a Keynesian and accept it.

3.2 Rules: abstract and general – specific and particular

Very similar considerations apply to Hayek's view that the market functions through the legal protection of individual 'domains'. In Nozick's case, the boundaries of these 'personal spaces' are marked out by the 'natural rights' we (allegedly) have, including the right to private property. For Hayek, on the other hand, they are demarcated by abstract, general, rules which have evolved over long periods. To qualify as abstract and general a rule must, on Hayek's account, be 'independent of purpose and be the same, if not necessarily for all members, at least for whole classes of members not individually designated by name' and it must be 'applicable to an unknown and indeterminable number of persons and instances' (1982: 50). Familiar moral rules such as 'keep promises' and 'don't tell lies', which match these criteria closely, are good examples. They apply to everyone, irrespective of who they may be, and, out of the enormous range of possibilities, it is impossible to predict the precise shape of the situations to which they apply which will actually materialise.

Note that Hayek's way of specifying abstractness and generality suggests various criteria according to which rules may be differentiated. For example, it may be possible to distinguish them in terms of the degree to which they exhibit these qualities; some rules being more abstract and general, others less so. Again, it suggests that there may be another class of rules with which the abstract and general may be contrasted: call these 'specific and particular' rules.

So, with this in mind, let us now consider how seriously Hayek's thesis is threatened by the possibility of there being such a thing as a class with only one member; the class of 'persons whose fingerprints show a particular pattern, definable by a certain algebraic formula' (Hayek's example; 1982: 35) or 'the class of world famous Austrian economists called F.A. Hayek' (my own). It is noticeable that where Hayek considers this at all, he dismisses it as irrelevant with a curt remark or two; for example, that 'What is meant by the term abstract is expressed in a classical juridical formula that states that the rule must apply to an unknown number of future instances' (1982: 35). But the trouble with this kind of response is that it completely misses the point. The point is that even classes which only contain one member – in fact and so far as we know, that is – potentially contain more. It follows that even the very specific rules just cited 'apply to an unknown number of future instances' and match the juridical formula Hayek cites. For example, although it is true that *for all we know* no two people have the same fingerprints, this doesn't rule out the possibility of there being two, however remote it may be. Or, what if time is cyclical and history repeats itself infinitely right down to the last detail? There would then be an infinite number of future F.A. Hayeks, identical in every respect, including date of birth, to the 'present' one. The speculation may be fanciful, but that is neither here nor there. It is sufficient to demonstrate that Hayek's thesis is, in at least one way, empty. Since it has to be true of *all* rules that they are 'applicable to an unknown and indeterminable number of persons and instances', it follows that there can be *no such thing* as a class of 'specific and particular' rules with which to contrast the abstract and general.

Does this matter? The answer is, on the one hand not much, but on the other, a great deal. It depends which aspect of Hayek's argument one takes. On the one hand, the spontaneous order thesis itself – the credible core of his account – is not completely threatened. All the spontaneous order thesis requires is a distinction between rules in terms of their *relative* abstractness and generality. All it needs to do is stress that rules must exhibit these qualities to a high degree (that they must in fact – in the real, known world – apply to very large classes of members and to a huge number of possibilities, only some of which will actually be realised) if they are to fulfil their function as transmitters of information between individuals, each pursuing his or her own purposes. Such rules resemble 'general purpose tools'. Hayek writes: 'Like a knife or a hammer they have been shaped not with a particular purpose in view but because in this form rather than in some other form they have proved serviceable in a great variety of situations' (1982: 21). It seems fairly clear that the 'fingerprint' rule is not general enough to qualify for this description, and Hayek doesn't need to postulate a realm of (non-existent) specific and particular rules to make his point.

But although 'spontaneous order' itself remains safe other aspects of Hayek's argument are completely undermined by the objection. These include the overtly pro-Right, pro-capitalist arguments which – as I am claiming – are mere *addenda* and bear no real relation to his central thesis. Hayek's distinction between the spontaneous and the 'made' order is a case in point. It is the 'constructivist error', 'the fatal conceit that man is able to shape the world around him according to his wishes' of which socialism is supposed to be guilty (1988: 27). Hayek's argument here is that *whereas* the former is characterised by abstract and general rules, the latter rests ultimately upon *commands*. He writes, 'What distinguishes the rules which will govern action within an organisation is that they must be rules for the performance of assigned tasks', from which it is supposed to follow that 'Rules of organisation are thus necessarily subsidiary to commands, filling in the gaps left by the commands' (1982: 49).

So let us ask, what is supposed to be the difference between a spontaneously evolved rule and a command? One difference seems clear; only the latter is issued intentionally, with a purpose. Hayek stresses this, but it won't yield the conclusion he wants. He needs to show, as he says, that the two types of order are *necessarily* different, but the distinction won't help him show this because for any spontaneous order there could – conceivably if not practicably – be a constructed or 'made' substitute. What if Hayek – like Locke – had introduced God into his story? According to Locke, 'God, when he gave the World in common to all Mankind, *commanded* Man also to labour', and 'God and his [i.e. man's] Reason *commanded* him to subdue the Earth, i.e. improve it for the benefit of Life' (Locke 1988: 291) (emphasis mine). In Locke's version of things, then, those who proceeded to 'mix their labour' with nature, and so initiate the process which led in time to the full development of an economic system based on private property, were – even if blindly and unwittingly – obeying a command. One only has to vary this slightly to get a story according to which those who, by their actions if not their intentions, developed the spontaneous order were, similarly, unwittingly carrying out commands.

In this case the distinction between spontaneous and made orders in terms of command would disappear. The spontaneous order would itself be a made order, although I don't suppose Hayek would be led to entertain second thoughts on this score. It follows that he needs some other criterion for distinguishing types of order if he is to make his case, and this he supplies with an argument that the rules governing spontaneous and made orders differ not only in *origin* (being commands only in the latter case) but in *nature*. Thus, we are told that 'What distinguishes the rules which will govern action within an organisation is that they must be rules for the performance of assigned tasks', and that 'By contrast, the rules governing a spontaneous order must be independent of purpose' etc. (1982: 49, 50). In other words, it is Hayek's view that *whereas* the rules governing a spontaneous order are abstract and general, those governing a made order are not.

This cannot be right. The made order may originate in a command, but it can't follow that its rules – being commands (now in a different sense of 'command') – fall into some 'non-abstract', 'non-general' ('specific and particular') category. There is no such category. Hayek's argument gains any plausibility it has only because an ambiguity in 'command' enables him to slide sideways between conclusions.

3.3 Domains

Such considerations add further support to the conclusion that there are two Hayeks. One, the modest and imaginative social theorist, has the following piece of good advice to offer: 'The market is a delicate mechanism with an important function. It doesn't always work, and sometimes you do have to adjust and modify its working, but always take care and try to be sure what you're doing when you try' (I paraphrase). This is advice which many, including many on the Left, will find no difficulty in accepting or even echoing. 'We are no longer in search of an alternative economic system' says (the definitely non-libertarian) J.K. Galbraith when addressing a meeting of the British Labour Party, and 'We are concerned with making more effective and more tolerant and equitable the economic system we have' (Galbraith 1992). Hayek can agree, and he would also agree that our ability to think, judge, weigh consequences and so on is itself the outcome of evolution. It is the mechanism we humans have developed for adapting to the contingencies our environment throws up (unlike bees, who can rely on instinct). Note that, since this advice doesn't even tell us *when* it is advisable to leave well alone and when it is permissible to 'interfere', one conclusion clearly *not* entailed by the spontaneous order thesis is that we would be well-advised to trust in the invisible hand.

The other Hayek is Hayek the libertarian; Hayek the paranoid and splenetic reactionary; the Hayek who fulminates against his pet hates – 'the counter-culture', 'permissive education', 'dropouts', 'parasites' and so on – like any dyspeptic ten-a-penny rednecked blimp (Hayek 1982: 174; 1988: 152). This Hayek is unconnected with the former, and should be ignored.

As a last example of how the difference between the two can be obscured, consider the systematic ambiguity which pervades the following (highly characteristic) passage.

> The chief function of rules of just conduct is thus to tell each what he can count upon, what material objects or services he can use for his purposes, and what is the range of actions open to him. . . . The rules of just conduct thus delimit protected domains not by directly assigning particular things to particular persons, but by making it possible to derive from ascertainable facts to whom particular things belong.
>
> (Hayek 1982: 37)

Every key term Hayek employs here – 'rule of just conduct', 'domain', even 'belong' – carries a dual interpretation. We get one interpretation if we take the passage to be a statement of Hayek's central spontaneous order thesis. We get quite another if we take it to be stating a fundamental article of the libertarian faith. Recall that, if Hayek is to stand where he wants to stand – on the Right and somewhere in the vicinity of Nozick – it has to follow from his main argument that his 'protected domains' are more or less equivalent in area to Nozick's rights-protected 'personal spaces'. The rules which define the domains must be equivalent to rules which define private (as opposed to, say, collective) property within the context of a free market, capitalist economic system.

But none of this can be shown, thanks to the essentially instrumental character of the spontaneous order argument. As we have seen, although the spontaneous order has no purpose, it certainly fulfils a number of functions, and the 'rules of just conduct' which have evolved have (supposedly) maintained their prominence because they are the ones which best serve those functions. However, this story does nothing to provide what Hayek requires; the *guarantee* that those rules will bear any recognisable relationship to the rules which govern capitalism. If it looks that way, that can only be thanks to facts such as the following: (1) *Any* rule – being a rule – tells 'each what he can count upon, what material objects or services he can use for his purpose, and what is the range of actions open to him'; (2) It therefore assigns rights of control to individuals, and in *that* sense, but only in that sense, assigns property rights. (A right of control may or may not amount to what one might normally want to count as a property right, of course.) (3) This being so, the rule evidently delimits protected *domains*, and since – of necessity – it assigns them to individuals there is, (4) a very obvious sense of 'private' in which those domains are *private*.

Now, it is certainly conceivable that, in the course of its evolution, the spontaneous order might throw up a collective rule – a 'rule of sharing'. A rule governing the use joint or collective owners make of their refrigerator might be an example. Such a rule would tell 'each what he can count upon, what material objects he can use', it would delimit domains and so on, but a society in which this type of rule was predominantly operative would be absolutely unrecognisable as capitalist.

Here – and yet again – we see Hayek buying credibility at the cost of indeterminacy, so much so that a genuine defence of the free market, in line with libertarian ideals, cannot be derived from his spontaneous order thesis. It may even be that taking 'spontaneous order' seriously means treating the phrase 'free market' itself as ambiguous (in line with the ambiguity of the 'domains' which define the market rights of market agents). And the situation isn't helped either by the fact that the 'rules of just conduct' which defined property are held to do so in a way which

construes 'property' widely, to include 'property in the person'. For
example, some libertarians hold that equal opportunities legislation, designed to protect women's working conditions, constitutes interference
with the market, and that, as Hayek would say, it deprives individuals 'of
the possibility of using their knowledge for their own ends' (1982: 51).[4] But
the alternative view, that such legislation – like legislation against slavery
– protects property in the person, that it represents an 'endeavour to
improve the spontaneous order by revising the rules on which it rests' is
just as consistent with Hayek's theory.

4 EVOLUTIONISM'S OTHER FACE

There is a darker and more sinister aspect to Hayek's evolutionism, and
it only remains to comment on this. Two points are relevant here. First,
whereas there is good scientific evidence to support the theory of evolution
in biology there is nothing corresponding to this in the case of Hayek's
theory. In the case of the former, experiments have tended to confirm that
the evolutionary *mechanism* – the selection and random mutation of DNA
in other words – actually operates.[5] This evidence is quite independent of
the fossil record, which simply illustrates what the results of the mechanism's operation have turned out to be in a particular case (Earth's). There
ought to be something analogous to this within Hayek's evolutionistic
social theory; that is, evidence that non-interference with the spontaneous
order produces optimal results. Moreover, this evidence ought to be
independent of the historical record which simply describes which 'orders'
have actually tended to predominate over time. But there is nothing
analogous. By contrast, the only reason we have for believing that non-interference is best is the spontaneous order story itself, and this – of course
– is to presuppose the theory rather than confirm it. What this means is
that to follow Hayek by placing faith in the market is just that; *faith* and
nothing more.

Second, evolution has left us with physiological hangovers, 'vestigial'
organs, such as the appendix, which may have been useful to our primate
ancestors but which do nothing for us. It is Hayek's view that – likewise –
the evolution of morality has left us with some out-of-date attitudes. As he
puts it, 'Our present moral views undoubtedly still contain layers or strata
deriving from earlier phases of the evolution of human societies' (1982:
142). This could be true, but it ought to be obvious that we have absolutely
no way of determining which of our attitudes are the outmoded ones. One
might expect Hayek to have realised this, but in fact it doesn't stop him
from leaving us in no doubt as to which he thinks they are. They are the

moral attitudes left over from the days of 'hunter-gatherer' society, the ones appropriate to the 'closed' group or tribe and hence – in his view – to be identified with 'collectivism' and the welfare state. 'Survival', according to Hayek, dictates the rejection of these in favour of 'open' market values.

So it turns out, after all, that Hayek's theory and Nozick's have much in common. Like Nozick's, Hayek's adds up to little more than a rhetorical gesture of faith in the free market, and, like Nozick's, Hayek's tries to persuade us to revise our morality in a particular direction. One function of 'spontaneous order' is to serve as a grandiose rhetorical prop for this attempt. And just as one can recount a Nozickian, so one can tell a Hayekian version of the Good Samaritan parable. It runs as follows: A Samaritan came across a victim and helped him to an inn, as in the original. It then adds: What a terrible example! This Samaritan was prey to primitive 'hunter-gatherer' urges when he 'had the opportunity to exploit special circumstances' and 'the possibility to do so profitably' (1982: 117).

Still, we need take no notice. 'Spontaneous order' may have a certain breathtaking narrative sweep but – like the Fable of the Bees – it's just a story.[6]

Chapter 12

Conclusions and postscript

The general conclusion I draw is that neither of the two main strategies open to libertarianism can hope to succeed. There is no real foundation for a rights-based intuitionism (such as Nozick's), and a conventionalist consequentialism (like Hayek's) could conceivably justify something quite different from the capitalist free market. The libertarian defence of a pure free market based on the institution of private property must therefore be judged a failure.

Otherwise: I am sure that many readers will recognise the type of experience Peter Ackroyd's encounter with Dickens evoked; the experience of being brought graphically face-to-face with some mysterious detail of an age now vanished. I was similarly confronted by the past on a recent occasion when my father related how, as a small child, he used to take lunch to his father. This was one of his many domestic duties. It seems that when the school bell rang for break, he would have to run home, collect the lunch from his mother and transport it (in a bowl covered by a handkerchief) to the cotton mill where my grandfather worked as a hand. These events took place in the 1920s in industrial Lancashire. I try to picture this. Images I cannot escape are as follows: small hands; a warm bowl, growing colder; hard winter streets; an infant finding his way through a machine shop; the menace of danger – I know that spindles could sometimes break loose from their looms, like drunken, malicious harpoons; clattering noise. ('A Modern Weaving Shed, in intensity of clatter from hundreds of rapidly working looms, is a pandemonium in which gossip by voice is impossible' writes one contemporary observer, adding that 'Jove the thunderer could not make himself heard in the din' (Pendleton 1902: 290).) Above all, there is what must have been the anxiety of it; the hasty rush from school to home to factory, and then back to school again in time for class. When I try, I end up by imagining events so foreign to me, so different from anything my own life has ever shown me, that they might as well have taken place in some remote country I have never visited. And yet the real wonder – the true source of the eerie feeling this kind of time-traveller's tale can generate – is not just that; it is the knowledge that the child in the machine shop is the very same person one thinks one knows so well; the one telling the story. How can this person have managed to get all the way from there to here?

I realise that, in its details, my account may be a little inexact and partial – I'll never know for sure – but I'm absolutely confident that the way I imagine my father's experience to have been does nothing to falsify or sentimentalise it. Sentiment and nostalgia have no place here; although I am aware that anyone writing about this sort of thing in the 1990s, when images of small boys in northern towns are use by advertisers to sell bread, runs the risk of evoking only that. Such soft-focus imagery disguises hard realities, a fact which becomes perfectly apparent once one starts to contemplate what must have been the general features of the environment within which these events took place.

First, there was the poverty. It's obvious that times were pretty hard for my father and for children like him. (After all, this was a time of economic depression.) Second, it is evident that the poverty was compounded by an absence of ameliorative features; features which would be taken for granted by generations arriving only slightly later. Was there a canteen at my grandfather's place of work? It seems not. Was there a caring schoolteacher, specially responsible for keeping a pastoral eye on the duty-burdened child? Again, it seems not. On the contrary, it would have been taken for granted in those days that one should shoulder one's burden – one's 'own' burden – and bear it. (This was a time when belief 'in the desirability of caring for children within a family rather than an institutional environment became . . . firmly established' (Thane 1982: 200).) A third feature, that my father's childhood world was riven with inequality, is brought home to me not so much by the story itself but by its contrast with a photograph I know. This features another small child taken at around the same age. The child, my common-law-father-in-law, is pictured between two servants, poised precariously on the back of an elephant as it strides the shallow waters of a Burmese river. (No one can seriously regret the passing of the world *that* icon represents either.) Still, the inequality *in itself* is not the point, and – as I have said – I am unimpressed by envy. But those who glibly claim to find nothing at all wrong with inequality might care to reflect – as I frequently do – that had the two men met as children they would probably have been completely incomprehensible to one another. Such mutual incomprehension is just one effect inequality can have. I find it hard to believe that there is nothing to be said against a set up which renders it possible.

Now, there would be no point in describing my father's experience if it were in any way exceptional. Rather, the point lies in its typicality. In the 1920s 'a very high proportion of children selected for grammar schools refused the places offered. . . .Parents could not afford the obligatory uniform of such schools, nor could they afford to forego the child's earnings to the age of sixteen' (Thane 1982: 201). There you have the explanation for the hard hours my grandfather worked, the consequent infrequency of contact with his son, the inequality of opportunity. My father's story only serves as a reminder that facts expressed as generalisations by historians and sociologists mean a real cost in someone's experience.

But, to continue, so far as I am concerned the worst aspect of my father's childhood situation was not its poverty, nor its harshness, nor the inequality it exemplified. It was – fourthly – what must have then seemed its permanence. There would have been a general absence of the idea that there might be other possibilities, that one might do or become more, that things might be arranged differently so that – for example – children from northern towns and children who get to ride elephants might occasionally communicate with understanding. So, if you want an image which encapsulates the way I take my father's childhood to have been, I guess it has to be this: A street extending in a straight line to infinity; a child, with his bowl, running for ever. This child is not going to look up at the sky, nor does it look likely that he will even think to do so.

But the street did not go on forever, and the child did look up. How come? According to Richard Titmuss, 'the circumstances of the war created an unprecedented sense of social solidarity among the British people, which made them willing to accept a great increase of egalitarian policies and collective state intervention' (Thane 1982: 223).[1] That may or may not be an exaggeration and, in any case, I'm not claiming that Utopia was realised. One thing is clear, though. From around the beginning of the Second World War, and for a considerable period afterwards, political life throughout the West generally was leavened by a loosely egalitarian vision according to which there was such a thing as society and social life meant each individual taking some responsibility for the well-being of others. For a time, hope, as opposed to fear, came to fuel the social mechanism and – as I put it earlier – human beings with aspirations to autonomy sought to influence all aspects of their world in accordance with a whole range of values (or at least some did).[2] One result was possibilities of movement; so much so that many readers of this book would never have enjoyed the same opportunities, or have turned out to be anything like the individuals they are, had it not been for the influence of that vision.

Will this book have a happy ending, then? Of course it won't, thanks to the way the post-war vision has been insidiously undermined by a meaner, narrower view of things over recent years. Economic hard times are back too. There are newer streets to walk, but they are bleak streets all the same. It is libertarianism – 'anti-libertarianism' as we should now more accurately begin to call it – which represents this betrayal at the theoretical level. So let me bring things to a close, as follows, by listing a few of the main reasons I hold the doctrine in such contempt.

First, there is the way libertarianism attempts to reconcile us to the new hard times – to the harsher effects of the market's unameliorated operation – by portraying them as somehow noble and unavoidably right. It is a tasteless and self-satisfied manoeuvre which is worse than simply philosophically unsustainable. Second, there is the way it holds market values – 'efficiency' and so forth – to be the ultimate moral benchmark in all walks of life, thus bumptiously inflating them and insinuating them into areas where they have no place (by demoting citizens and patients to the status of 'customer', for example). Third, there is the way it represents a return to the free market as a universal panacea. I despise this for the way it blocks out and stultifies real, problem-solving thought. Fourth, and libertarianism's worst feature by far, there is its own, especially characteristic, resort to nostalgia. While caricaturing the post-war changes as, at the very least, a great mistake and as, at worst, no better than Stalinism, it attempts to persuade us that a return to a cold, cruel, class-ridden world resembling that of the 1920s and 1930s would, in reality, resemble the setting up of some cosy version of small town America. It is for this that I hate it most. Such a world has probably never even existed outside the imaginations of Rothbard, Nozick, Norman Rockwell and Walt Disney.

Finally, and naturally enough, I wonder what we will find ourselves telling those who come after us, our own children and grandchildren, when they ask us what it was like. Will the world we describe seem as strange to them as Dickens's did to Ackroyd or my father's to me? Will we find ourselves saying: 'You're not going to believe this, but once we could fly like angels'? If we do, will they react only with incredulity? I hope they don't have to. They deserve better.

Notes

1 Libertarianism – anti-libertarianism

1 For a thorough synoptic account, readers could do worse than consult Shand 1990.

2 The quotations are from the No Turning Back Group of Conservative MPs (1990: 8, 14). The contents of this pamphlet are fairly typical of the way watered-down libertarian ideas are employed as propaganda.

3 Sir Keith Joseph was Secretary of State for Trade and Industry from 1979 to 1982; that is, during the first Thatcher government's early, more optimistic, and ideologically loaded period. Seeking to re-educate the civil servants in his charge, one of his first acts on taking office was to distribute a reading list throughout the ministry. One of the items on the list was a book he co-authored with Jonathan Sumption (Joseph and Sumption 1979). For the full list, and a clear, non-committal, summary of its contents, readers should consult Bosanquet (1981). Sir Keith is now president of the (libertarian) Institute of Economic Affairs.

4 See, for example, the title of Antony Flew's critique of egalitarianism, *The Politics of Procrustes* (1981). Procrustes also gets a mention from Sir Keith (Joseph and Sumption 1979: 63). The myth goes: 'Procrustes used to welcome travellers, feast them and give them a bed for the night. He had only one bed, and if the visitors were too long for it he cut off their legs to make them fit; if they were too short he put them on a rack to lengthen them' (McLeish 1983: 252).

5 In his essay, 'Bentham', John Stuart Mill wrote, 'For our own part, we have a large tolerance for one-eyed men' (1987). Jonathan Wolff quotes this in approval of Nozick (1991: 142).

2 Market romances I: nuts and bolts

1 Although much of this book concentrates on the conceptual analysis of freedom, I haven't thought it necessary to carry out a detailed analysis of coercion. For a detailed analysis by a notable libertarian see Nozick (1972). For a detailed anti-libertarian account see Haworth (1990).

2 The True Levellers, or Diggers (1649–59), had a habit of seizing common land and sharing it out. Their manifesto, *The True Levellers' Standard Advanced*

states, for example, that 'the earth, which was made to be a common treasury of relief for all, both beasts and men, was hedged into enclosures by the teachers and rulers, and the others were made servants and slaves', and 'that earth that is within this creation made a common storehouse for all, is bought and sold and kept in the hands of a few; whereby the great Creator is mightily dishonoured' (quoted in Woodhouse 1938: 379).

3 For example, the No Turning Backers make great play of their claim to be giving people 'greater responsibility for their own lives'. The reduction of entitlement to state support, which they call 'the extension of choice', is described by them as something 'which actually widens, not diminishes, care and responsibility' (No Turning Back Group of Conservative MPs 1990: 7, 12).

3 Reducibility, freedom, the invisible hand

1 In the case of both quotations, the italics are mine.

2 See Hobbes (1985). The cover of the present Penguin edition is a representation of the famous original. Let's hope they keep it that way.

3 Libertarians tend to interpret Locke in a way congenial to their own view. However, it seems to me that there are other interpretations, far less in line with libertarianism and far more in line with my view. See, for example, Ryan (1984). Ryan writes: 'To see Locke as no more than an apologist for capitalism is ludicrous' (1984: 48). Throughout the period in which I have been writing this book, and in which I have as a consequence been constrained to pay some attention to Locke, I have become increasingly convinced that Ryan is right (see also Ryan (1965)).

4 'Entitlement' and 'holding' are Nozick's terms. According to Nozick, a just distribution results from the repeated application over time of a 'principle of justice in acquisition' and a 'principle of justice in transfer'. For this, see especially Nozick (1974: 150ff).

5 Hayek is obviously using 'men' to include women here. I suppose this was forgivable in 1960 (and I am afraid that I regard it as important to quote things exactly as they are written). Feminists and others likely to be offended by this sort of thing might be interested to learn that, in later years, Hayek dropped this usage in favour of something less sexist. See, for example, Hayek (1988).

6 For a full and thorough treatment of equality – one with which, by the way, I am strongly in sympathy – readers should consult Baker (1987).

7 A recent, and illuminating, account of the relation between wealth and power in a capitalist economy is Bowles and Gintis (1992).

8 The quotations are from Hayek's essay 'Economic Freedom and Representative Government' (first published in 1973). This is one of the essays included in Hayek (1978: 117). Hayek's views on democracy are more fully elaborated in Hayek (1978).

9 I say 'typically placed' because there may well be highly bizarre situations to which what I say here does not apply. I must admit that I can't think of any examples.

10 For another subtle and interesting treatment of this problem see Lloyd-Thomas (1988).

4   Market romances II: love is strange

1   Rothbard writes: 'It so happens that the free-market economy . . . is by far the most productive form of economy known to man.' This leaves it unclear whether he regards the invisible hand thesis as strictly entailed by the reducibility thesis or whether this is, as he goes on to say, simply 'a fortunate utilitarian result of the free market' (1973: 40). Nevertheless, it seems to me that – underlying his arguments – there is the view that the entailment does hold. For a start, the remarks quoted immediately precede the 'newsvendor' passage, which is designed to show how market exchanges work out to the advantage of all involved. Also, I doubt that Rothbard could be so enthusiastic over the market's alleged virtues if, as he doesn't think, it were to turn out to be seriously unproductive. Similar considerations apply to Nozick. *Anarchy, State, and Utopia* wouldn't yield a convincing defence of the free market unless it were the case that the great majority of exchanges were 'productive' in his sense (1974: 84–6).

2   I use the word 'morally' loosely here. The features I outline in this paragraph are shared by many types of evaluative term. They are shared by the terms of evaluation we employ in aesthetic matters, for example. 'Morally' is intended to cover these as well. I'm not entirely happy with 'morally', but I can't think of a better, so 'morally' will have to do.

3   Hayek quotes Mandeville approvingly in *The Fatal Conceit* (1988: 12–13). The passage can be found in Mandeville (1970: 68). See also Hayek's essay, 'Dr Bernard Mandeville' (1966), reprinted in Hayek (1978: 249–66).

4   Thus, the No Turning Backers write, 'We proclaim unequivocally our belief in the family as the building block of society' (No Turning Back Group of Conservative MPs 1990: 12). For an interesting recent account of the Right's attitude to family values see Somerville (1992).

5   Two classic texts are Burke (1968) and Oakeshott (1962).

5   On freedom

1   The other two 'confusions of individual liberty with different concepts' to which Hayek refers here are what he calls 'political freedom' (participation in the choice of government) and what he calls 'inner' or 'metaphysical' freedom.

2   Flew comments: ' "The free man", wrote the French *philosophe* Helvetius, "is the man who is not in irons, nor imprisoned in a gaol, nor terrorised like a slave by fear of punishment" . . . "it is not lack of freedom not to fly like an eagle or swim like a whale" ' (1978: 156). This echoes a footnote of Berlin's: 'Helvetius made this point very clearly: "The free man is the man who is not" ' etc. (1969: 122n). It seems to me that one way to measure the degree to which some given writer is influenced by Berlin can be measured with the help of this 'Helvetius factor'. For example, consider Sir Keith Joseph, who, with characteristic originality, points out that ' "It is not lack of freedom not to fly like an eagle or swim like a whale", said Helvetius' (Joseph and Sumption 1979: 48).

3   Machan's remark is directly aimed at a comment of my own, that 'if I arrive at the supermarket only to find that you have just purchased the last tin of

beans then, and as a result of your action, I am rendered unfree to buy beans there', which was intended to illustrate the point that 'the normal exercise of property rights within the context of a free market can obviously result in an individual's becoming negatively unfree to perform some specific action' (Haworth 1989: 103). This makes it clear that his intention is to criticise 'my sort' of view.

4   This means that I won't be able to say enough to satisfy all readers who wish to raise objections or demand further points of clarification. I'm sure some will as I've written on this subject before (see Haworth 1991). I had thought of adding an appendix on freedom, but that would have made the book too long. Instead, some of the notes to this chapter do rather more work than is usual for notes.

5   Joel Feinberg writes of the thousands of New Yorkers who play illegal poker every night that they are unfree when viewed from a 'juridical perspective' but free when viewed from a 'sociological perspective' (1980: 7). Can't it be argued, similarly, that A is – maybe – unfree when viewed from a 'subjective perspective' but free when viewed from an 'objective perspective'? The answer is that it can, if like Feinberg one takes a 'single-schema' view of freedom according to which what counts as a constraint is a matter of perspective (or like Gerald C. MacCallum Jnr who makes it a matter of 'interpretation' (MacCallum 1972)). But this single-schema view is, to put it in my terms, a form of 'weak' negativism. Strong negativism has to rely on the presence or absence of genuine obstacles, and these obstruct from *any* perspective. (For a fuller account of this, see Haworth (1991)).

6   Berlin is guilty of a tautology compounded by a *non sequitur* here. Thus, Berlin is free to define 'political' liberty as he likes; that is, he can make it true *by definition* that 'political' liberty can only be compromised or violated by the deliberate interference of another person or persons (hence the tautology). But then nothing would follow from this definition for freedom in general. But it is quite clear from the fact that Berlin goes on to discuss 'economic freedom' and 'economic slavery' in the very same paragraph that he does intend the qualification to carry implications for these.

7   It seems to me that *norms* have a role to play here. The contrast between the paraplegic and the 'normally' able person may, thus, go some way to explaining why it is in some way correct to describe the former as lacking the freedom to walk. Of course, norms can change. As I go on to say, if space travel were ever to become usual even gravity might start to look like an obstacle to freedom.

8   For a full account of Hayek's view, see Chapter 11.

9   I'm not entirely happy with the phrase 'ownership model' because it suggests the very connection I am concerned to deny between ownership of one's actions and – on the other hand – an economic system based on the private ownership of possessions. Still, 'authorship model' doesn't seem right either; so I'll stick to 'ownership model'.

10 However, I'll just add that, in my view, *something like* the view of freedom developed by Harry G. Frankfurt Jnr in his 'Freedom of the Will and the Concept of a Person' (1971) is right, or at least capable of capturing some of the phenomena. Frankfurt's distinction between 'first order' and 'second order' desires does more justice than negativism to what is distinctive about

human action. Nor can I see any reason why Frankfurt's bifurcation of the self should be spurious, or why his 'second order desires' should necessarily be equated with something more sinister. For writers such as Berlin, these are the characteristic vices of 'positive' accounts of freedom.

11 For a good introduction to these problems see Singer (1979).

6 The legend of the angels and the fable of the bees

1 The lines quoted are from Hayek (1960: 16) and Nozick (1974: 262). (See also p. 39–40 above.)

2 Plato's philosopher rulers were professional liars, of course. Note that I am absolutely not accusing libertarian writers of any such dishonesty. I just mean exactly what I say, that since 'the fable has a role to play within a certain political vision' it is interesting to consider what one might find oneself saying if one were to try to persuade people they were bees. I stress this because some libertarian writers don't seem to be able to tell the difference between deliberately 'bamboozling' the reader and, on the other hand, honestly making assumptions which carry rhetorical (as opposed to argumentative) force. For an example see Machan (1989: 217).

3 Marx's classic writings on alienation are contained in Marx (1973).

7 Moralising the market

1 One of the best collections of writings centrally relevant to this issue is Glover (1990).

2 The phrase, 'the greatest good' suggests that all individual goods can be harmonised in some way. Libertarians are sceptical of this idea, and so am I.

3 For the classic statement of Kant's position see Kant (1948).

4 See p. 9ff.

8 Rights, wrongs and rhetoric

1 Locke's argument is backed up with an appeal to revelation, or, rather, an equally backhanded appeal to the lack of any relevant revelation. It is *not* the case that 'the Lord and Master of them all' has 'by any manifest declaration of his will set one above another' or conferred on him 'by an evident and clear appointment an undoubted right to dominion and sovereignty' (1988: 269). For Locke, we are God's property, and the injunction to exploit nature is in line with God's purposes for us. That we are 'his Property' and 'made to last during his, not one another's Pleasure' is another reason Locke gives for thinking that 'there cannot be supposed any such *Subordination* among us' (ibid.: 271); a reason which highlights still more just how different from each other the modern argument and Locke's are.

2 According to Williams, 'having sympathetic concern for others is a necessary condition of being in the world of morality'. I am sympathetic to his argument that if one takes the notion of 'the amoralist' seriously one ends up imagining someone who may not be 'recognisably human' (1972: 26, 23). However, I

don't think the argument I present here actually commits me to this view.

3   This version of the parable is to be found in the King James version, *The Gospel According to St Luke*, X, 30–36. I have no idea how much two pence was worth in real terms at the time the King James version was translated, but I think the context makes it clear that the sum was quite modest.

4   I am very likely to be misunderstood at this point, so let me stress that *nothing* hangs on whether I have interpreted the parable 'correctly'. (This is not an exercise in Biblical scholarship and, should you think it relevant, I am an atheist in any case.) My point is only that, being part of a longstanding and influential tradition, the parable carries certain weight. To suppose more – to treat the 'correct' interpretation as authoritatively decisive – would be to commit the same error as the intuitionist for whom 'intuition' is decisive.

Related points which may need even more emphasis than I have given them in the text – at least so far as some readers may be concerned – are as follows: (1) By 'natural' I mean 'unconstrained' here and, as I explain, by the 'natural interpretation' of the parable I mean the interpretation which would in this sense, 'come naturally' to a modern reader. (2) The 'natural' interpretation is in many ways different from the interpretation which would have come naturally to Christ's original audience. The latter would have been well aware of the long-running enmity between Jews and Samaritans, a context in which the Samaritan can only be seen as having done something highly unusual. Modern readers who know the parable may well be unaware of this context. (3) However, there is one crucial respect in which the 'ancient' and 'modern' interpretations are not so different. According to both, the Samaritan only does what is *morally expected* (which – for Christ's original audience – is what no one would have expected him to do). (4) This holds *whether or not* one also thinks the Samaritan would have been acting within his rights had he continued on his way.

5   Just to make sure that I am not misunderstood, let me repeat in this footnote that I do not think that Nozick has to treat insisting upon one's rights as morally exemplary in all circumstances. He writes: 'Note that we do not hold the nonviolation of our rights as our sole greatest good or even rank it first lexicographically to exclude trade-offs, if there is some desirable society we would choose to inhabit even though in it some rights of ours are violated, rather than move to a desert island where we could survive alone' (Nozick 1974: 28). But – note – his emphasis on 'trade-offs' and on *choosing* to remain where one is show that, as I am claiming, he treats entitlements as always taking priority. It is this I question. On this, see also Thomson (1977).

6   How capitalist is Nozick? Jonathan Wolff points out that Nozick's moral vision permits but does not strictly entail the recommendation of *laissez faire* capitalism. Libertarianism 'recommends nothing'. Moreover, individuals acting within their entitlements could choose to establish all manner of communities. In Utopia – as described by Nozick in Part III of his book – they could elect to leave one community to join another. Wolff is right – strictly speaking – but I don't think this affects my point which is that an ethical view which treats the right to property as a fundamental right (libertarianism) *lends itself* to the defence of an economic system which rests on freedom of exchange between owners of private property ('pure' capitalism). I also think, as Wolff goes on to point out, that in Nozick's Utopia

'the law of the survival of the economically most fit' would lead 'to a development not of diversity but of homogeneity' (Wolff 1991: 133ff).

7   If an untrained person tries to set up in business as a surgeon (without hiding his or her absence of qualifications) and if – further – that person manages to gain customers, can't Nozick argue that this should be prohibited on the grounds that this is a risky activity? It is not obvious that he can, if only because the customers would be consenting to the 'treatment' (see Nozick 1974: 57ff). Still, I am concentrating on Nozick's central metaphor here, although I suspect that some of the more technical parts of his argument tend to undermine that metaphor rather than support it. (On this see Wolff (1981) and Paul (1980).) Even if I'm wrong it doesn't make his argument against Williams any better.

8   See also Townsend (1989).

9   Bessie Smith was seriously injured in a road crash. She died after having been refused admission by a 'whites only' hospital. This was in Memphis in 1937

10 As with many British readers it was some time before I was able to appreciate the full force of Nozick's argument because I first had to find out who Wilt Chamberlain is.

9   Visions of Valhalla

1   For another example see Aarstol (1991). For my response see Haworth (1992).

2   At one time Wittgenstein planned to settle in Russia as a manual labourer. However, it has to be said that he took a rather rosy-spectacled view. In his brilliant biography of Wittgenstein, Ray Monk writes: 'Despite the fact that Wittgenstein was never at any time a Marxist, he was perceived as a sympathetic figure by the students who formed the core of the Cambridge Communist Party. . . . But Wittgenstein's reasons for wanting to visit Russia were very different. His perception of the decline of the countries of Western Europe was always more Spenglerian than Marxian, and . . . it is likely that he was extremely attracted to the portrait of life in the Soviet Union drawn by Keynes in his *Short View of Russia* – a portrait which, while deprecating Marxism as an economic theory, applauded its practice in Russia as a new religion, in which there were no supernatural beliefs but, rather, deeply held religious attitudes' (Monk 1990: 348).

3   I am not forgetting the 'Lecture on Ethics'; but in this Wittgenstein argues that ethics is a futile activity, an attempt to formulate 'what cannot be said' in words. (The lecture is reprinted in *The Philosophical Review*, 1965.)

4   In a famous sentence, Laslett wrote: 'For the moment anyway, political philosophy is dead' (Laslett 1956: vii). I leave aside the question of how it can be in line with 'ordinary usage' to describe something as dead 'for the moment anyway'.

5   I have found Stewart's book an invaluable help in writing this one.

6   Nozick doesn't say so explicitly, but it seems clear that he is assuming, not just that typical market exchanges respect the proviso, but that they are characteristically 'productive' in the sense that they leave both parties better off. To put it in my terms, he assumes the truth of that version of the reducibility thesis according to which the market just is the sum total of productive exchanges. He is therefore an optimist about the effects of

capitalism, as are other libertarians who overtly endorse the invisible hand thesis (see Nozick 1974: 84–6).

7   I suppose it may be arguable that very high levels of unemployment are quite tolerable, provided that the figure of however many unemployed it may be represents a different group of individuals each week. In this case, the individuals will be spending a short spell in the 'pool' before successfully finding other work. I am not now assuming any such optimistic scenario.

8   For Nozick's definition of the state see Nozick (1974: 23).

9   With the general conclusion he draws in Part I of *Anarchy, State, and Utopia* that the minimal state – if no other – is justified.

10   Smith writes: 'The third and last duty of the sovereign of commonwealth is that of erecting and maintaining those public institutions and those public works which, though they may be in the highest degree advantageous to a great society, are, however, of such a nature, that the profit could never repay the expense to any individual, and which it therefore cannot be expected that any individual or small number of individuals should erect or maintain' (1976: 244).

11   Huge problems arise thanks to the fact that medicine is becoming ever more sophisticated. More people can be treated, more diseases prevented, and so on. Whose needs should take priority? What are 'needs'? Shouldn't more priority be given to preventive measures and so on? But this just means that lines are difficult to draw. (The baldness/non-baldness problem, only worse.) It doesn't follow that the market will draw them any better, or that we should give up trying. In short, I disagree with Lomasky (1981).

12   For example, it won't satisfy those who think private education remains much as Orwell described it in 1941, 'a sort of tax that the middle classes pay to the upper class in return for the right to enter certain professions', or that the perpetuation of 'festering centres of snobbery' is not just undesirable in itself, but disastrously inefficient in its general economic consequences (Orwell 1970: 121).

10   The good fairy's wand

1   For a good example see Friedman and Friedman (1980: Chapter 3).

11   Hayek and the hand of fate

1   *Is* it true of a biological organism that, as with the lattice, 'we can learn from our acquaintance with some spatial or temporal part of the whole to form correct expectations concerning the rest' (1982: 36)? I wonder. Mightn't someone who tried to do this resemble the tic, with its head buried within the skin of the elephant, who tried to formulate a correct description of the elephant on the basis of its limited knowledge? Maybe it will be true when we know more about DNA. Still, it doesn't really matter. Hayek's thesis only requires the claim to be true for *some* 'orders'.

2   See for example Hayek (1982: 22–4). If Hayek is right then it is no accident that Hayek's distinction between 'made' and 'spontaneous' orders is mirrored more or less precisely in accounts of evolution, in Richard Dawkins's contrast

between William Paley's 'watch' argument and his own account of the origins of the bat, for example (see Dawkins 1986: esp. Chapter 1).

3   In 1979 Hayek had only just become acquainted with Rawls's work, and he wrote approvingly that 'the differences between us seemed more verbal than substantial' (Hayek 1982: iii). However, by 1988 Hayek felt able to dismiss Rawls's work as counter-evolutionary (see Hayek 1988: 74–5). It is a pity that Hayek was so dismissive.

4   In a characteristically libertarian – not to say Hayekian – tract it has recently been argued that equal opportunities legislation to counter discrimination against women constitutes 'more extensive interference with, and regulation of, the spontaneous workings of the free market'. Such legislation is held to 'undermine justice' because it weakens 'the institutions of private property, freedom of contract, and equality before the law'. State funded child-care is thus condemned on the grounds that 'those forced into paying for it lose their freedom to choose what to do with their income' (Nozick-style 'forced labour', in other words). None of this need follow, even from Hayekian premises, if the unfreedoms and inequalities which result from the market's operation are construed as violations of the property women hold in their persons (see Quest 1992: Introduction).

5   For example, there is nothing in Hayek's work to parallel Kettlewell's renowned systematic work on the peppered moth *biston betularia* (see Roberts 1971: 603).

6   Two recent books on Hayek which I have found especially helpful are Gray (1984) and Kukathas (1989).

12 Conclusions and postscript

1   See also Titmuss (1950).

2   Although Hayek spent an enormous amount of time and energy trying to demonstrate that 'social justice' is a 'mirage', I haven't wasted my time trying to tackle his view in detail. Hayek may well be right to suppose that there is no formula in terms of which the concept can be easily summarised. (If there were, I expect it would have been discovered ages ago.) But it seems to me that Hayek completely misrepresents the role values play in social and political life.

Bibliography

Note: To keep this bibliography manageable, I've simply listed the books and articles to which I actually refer in the text or in the notes. Dates of editions used appear in brackets and, where appropriate, dates of original publication appear in square brackets.

Aarstol, Michael (1991) 'Coercion, Aggression, and Capitalism', *Economy and society*, Vol. 20, No. 4: 402–10.

Ackroyd, Peter (1990) *Dickens*, London: Minerva.

Austin, J.L. (1970) [1956] 'A Plea for Excuses', in Urmson, J.O. and Warnock, G.J. (eds) *J.L. Austin, Philosophical Papers*, Oxford: Oxford University Press.

Baker, John (1987) *Arguing for Equality*, London: Verso.

Becker, Lawrence C. (1977) *Property Rights, Philosophic Foundations*, London: Routledge & Kegan Paul.

Berlin, Sir Isaiah (1969) [1958] 'Two Concepts of Liberty', in Berlin, Sir Isaiah, *Four Essays on Liberty*, Oxford: Oxford University Press.

Bosanquet, N. (1981) 'Sir Keith's reading list', *The Political Quarterly*, Vol. 52: 324–41.

Bowles, Samuel and Gintis, Herbert (1992) 'Power and Wealth in a Competitive Capitalist Economy', *Philosophy & Public Affairs*, Vol. 21, No. 4: 324–53.

Burke, Edmund, (1968) [1790] *Reflections on the Revolution in France*, O'Brien, Conor Cruise (ed.), London: Penguin.

Cohen, G.A. (1979) 'Capitalism, Freedom, and the Proletariat', in Ryan, Alan (ed.) *The Idea of Freedom*, Oxford: Oxford University Press.

Daniels, Norman (ed.) (1974) *Reading Rawls, Critical Studies of A Theory of Justice*, Oxford: Basil Blackwell.

Dawkins, Richard (1986) *The Blind Watchmaker*, London: Penguin.

Deutscher, Isaac (1966) *Stalin, A Political Biography*, London: Pelican.

Dworkin, Ronald (1977) *Taking Rights Seriously*, London: Duckworth.

Feinberg, Joel (1980) [1971] 'The Idea of a Free Man', in Feinberg, Joel *Rights, Justice, and the Bounds of Liberty*, Princeton, NJ: Princeton University Press.

Flew, Antony, (1978) 'The Philosophy of Freedom', in Watkins, K.W. (ed.) *In Defence of Freedom*, London: Cassell.

Flew, Antony (1981) *The Politics of Procrustes*, London: Temple Smith.

Frankfurt, Harry G. Jnr (1971) 'Freedom of the Will and the Concept of a Person', *Journal of Philosophy*, LXVIII: 5–20.

Friedman, Milton (1962) *Capitalism and Freedom*, Chicago: Chicago University Press.

Friedman, Milton and Friedman, Rose (1980) *Free to Choose*, London: Penguin.

Galbraith, J.K. (1992) 'Shifting gear, not direction' The *Guardian*, 25 November.

Glover, Jonathan (ed.) (1990) *Utilitarianism and Its Critics*, London: Macmillan.

Gray, John (1984) *Hayek on Liberty*, Oxford: Blackwell.

Hart, H.L.A. (1955) 'Are There any Natural Rights?', *Philosophical Review*, Vol. LXIV, No. 2; also in Waldron, Jeremy (ed.) (1984) *Theories of Rights*, Oxford: Oxford University Press.

Haworth, Alan (1989) 'Capitalism, Freedom, and Rhetoric: A Reply to Tibor R. Machan,' *Journal of Applied Philosophy*, Vol. 6, No. 1: 97–107.

Haworth, Alan (1990) 'What's So Special About Coercion?', *Economy and Society*, Vol. 19, No. 3: 376–89.

Haworth, Alan (1991) 'Models of Liberty: Berlin's "Two Concepts" ', *Economy and Society*, Vol. 20, No. 3: 245–59.

Haworth, Alan (1992) 'Coercion Revisited, or How to Demolish a Statue', *Economy and Society*, Vol. 21, No. 1: 75–90.

Hayek, F.A. (1944) *The Road to Serfdom*, London: Routledge & Kegan Paul.

Hayek, F.A. (1960) *The Constitution of Liberty*, London: Routledge & Kegan Paul.

Hayek, F.A. (1978) *New Studies in Philosophy, Politics, Economics, and the History of Ideas*, London: Routledge.

Hayek, F.A. (1982) *Law, Legislation, and Liberty* (One Volume Edition), London: Routledge.

Hayek, F.A. (1988) *The Fatal Conceit, The Errors of Socialism*, London: Routledge.

Hitler, Adolf (1969) [1925] *Mein Kampf*, London: Hutchinson.

Hobbes, Thomas (1985) [1651] *Leviathan*, ed. C.B. MacPherson, London: Penguin.

Honderich, T. (1990) *Conservatism*, London: Hamish Hamilton.

Huxley, Aldous (1946) [1932] *Brave New World*, London: Penguin.

Joseph, Keith and Sumption, Jonathan (1979) *Equality*, London: John Murray.

Kant, Immanuel (1948) [1785] *Groundwork of the Metaphysic of Morals*, trans. Paton, H.J. *The Moral Law*, London: Hutchinson.

Keynes, John Maynard (1973) [1936] *The General Theory of Employment, Interest and Money*, London: Macmillan/Cambridge University Press for the Royal Economic Society.

Kropotkin, Peter (1970) [1891] 'Anarchist Communism', in Baldwin, Roger N. (ed.) *Kropotkin's Revolutionary Pamphlets*, New York: Dover Publications.

Kukathas, Chandran (1989) *Hayek and Modern Liberalism*, Oxford: Oxford University Press.

Laslett, Peter (ed.) (1956) *Philosophy, Politics, and Society, First Series*, Oxford: Basil Blackwell.

Lloyd Thomas, David A. (1988) *In Defence of Liberalism*, Oxford: Basil Blackwell.

Locke, John (1964) [1690] *An Essay Concerning Human Understanding*, ed. Woozley, A.D., London: Collins, Fount.

Locke, John (1988) [1690] *Two Treatises of Government*, Student edition, ed. Laslett, Peter, Cambridge: Cambridge University Press.

Lomasky, Loren E. (1981) 'Medical Progress and Health Care', *Philosophy and Public Affairs*, Winter: 107–21; and in Machan, Tibor R. (ed.) (1982) *The Libertarian Reader*, New Jersey: Rowman & Littlefield.

MacCallum Jnr, Gerald, C. (1972) [1967] 'Negative and Positive Freedom', in Laslett, P., Runciman, W.G., and Skinner, Q. (eds) *Philosophy, Politics, and Society: Fourth Series*, Oxford: Blackwell.

Machan, Tibor R. (ed.) (1982) *The Libertarian Reader*, New Jersey: Rowman & Littlefield.

Machan, Tibor R. (1986) 'The Virtue of Freedom in Capitalism', *Journal of Applied Philosophy*, Vol. 3, No. 1: 49–58.

Machan, Tibor R. (1989) 'Capitalism, Freedom, and Rhetorical Argumentation', *Journal of Applied Philosophy*, Vol. 6, No. 2: 215–18.

Malcolm, Norman (1958) *Ludwig Wittgenstein, A Memoir*, Oxford: Oxford University Press.

Mandeville, Bernard (1970) [1705] 'The Grumbling Hive or, Knaves Turn'd Honest', in Harth, Phillip (ed.) *Mandeville, Bernard: The Fable of the Bees*, London: Penguin.

Mandeville, Bernard (1970) [1724] 'A Vindication of the Book from the Aspersions Contain'd in a Presentment of the Grand Jury of Middlesex', in Harth, Phillip (ed.) *Mandeville, Bernard: The Fable of the Bees*, London: Penguin.

Marx, Karl, (1973) [1844] *Economic and Philosophic Manuscripts of 1844*, ed. Struik, Dirk J., London: Lawrence & Wishart.

McLeish, Kenneth (1983) *Children of the Gods; The Complete Myths and Legends of Ancient Greece*, London: Longman.

Mill, John Stuart (1987) [1852] 'Whewell on Moral Philosophy', 'Utilitarianism' and 'Bentham' in Ryan, Alan. (ed.) Mill, John Stuart and Bentham, Jeremy, *Utilitarianism and Other Essays*, London: Penguin. (Originally published in the *Westminster Review* and reprinted a few years later in Mill's *Dissertations and Discussions*, Volume 2.)

Mill, John Stuart (1976) [1879] 'Chapters on Socialism', in Parry, Geraint (ed.) *John Stuart Mill on Politics and Society*, London: Fontana. (Originally published in *Fortnightly Review, New Series*, XXV.)

Millett, Kate (1972) *Sexual Politics*, London: Abacus.

Monk, Ray (1990) *Ludwig Wittgenstein, The Duty of Genius*, London: Jonathan Cape.

'No Turning Back' Group of Conservative MPs (1990) *Choice and Responsibility, The Enabling State*, London: Conservative Political Centre.

Nozick, Robert (1972) [1969] 'Coercion', in Laslett, P., Runciman, W.G., and Skinner, Q. (eds) *Philosophy, Politics, and Society: Fourth Series*, Oxford: Blackwell.

Nozick, Robert (1974) *Anarchy, State, and Utopia*, Oxford: Basil Blackwell.

Oakeshott, Michael (1962) *Rationalism in Politics and Other Essays*, London: Macmillan.

Orwell, George (1970) [1941] 'The lion and the unicorn', in Orwell, G. *Collected Essays, Journalism, and Letters*, London: Penguin.

Orwell, George (1968) [1944] 'Review of Hayek and Zilliacus', in Orwell, Sonia and Angus, Ian (eds) *The Collected Essays, Letters, and Journalism of George Orwell, Volume 3*, London: Penguin.

Paul, Jeffrey (ed.) (1981) *Reading Nozick: Essays on Anarchy, State, and Utopia*, Oxford: Basil Blackwell.

Pendleton, John (1902) 'Cotton at Port, in Mill, and on 'Change', *Britain at Work, A Pictoral Description of Our National Industries*, London: Cassell.

Plato (1987) [375BC] *The Republic*, trans. Lee, Desmond, London: Penguin.

Popper, Karl R. (1945) *The Open Society and its Enemies*, London: Routledge.

Quest, Caroline (ed.) (1992) *Equal Opportunities: A Feminist Fallacy*, London: IEA Health and Welfare Unit.

Rawls, John (1972) *A Theory of Justice*, Oxford: Clarendon Press.

Rawls, John (1985) 'Justice as Fairness: Political not Metaphysical', *Philosophy and Public Affairs*, Vol. 14, No. 3: 223–51.

Roberts, M.B.V. (1982) *Biology: A Functional Approach*, 3rd edn, London: Nelson.

Rothbard, Murray (1973) *For a New Liberty*, London: Macmillan.

Rothbard, Murray (1982) *The Ethics of Liberty*, New Jersey: Humanities Press.

Ryan, Alan (1965) 'Locke and The Dictatorship of the Bourgeoisie', *Political Studies*, Vol. XIII.

Ryan, Alan (1984) *Property and Political Theory*, Oxford: Basil Blackwell.

Scruton, Roger (1980) *The Meaning of Conservatism*, London: Penguin.

Shand, Alexander H. (1990) *Free Market Morality*, London: Routledge.

Sher, George (1983) 'Our Preferences, Ourselves', *Philosophy and Public Affairs*, Vol. 12, No. 1: 34–50.

Singer, Peter (1979) *Practical Ethics*, Cambridge: Cambridge University Press.

Smith, Adam (1976) [1776] *The Wealth of Nations* ed. Cannan, Edwin, Chicago: Chicago University Press.

Somerville, Jennifer (1992) 'The New Right and Family Politics', *Economy and Society*, Vol. 21, No. 2: 93–128.

Stewart, Michael (1986) *Keynes and After*, 3rd edn, London: Penguin.

Thane, Pat (1982) *The Foundations of the Welfare State*, London and New York: Longman.

Thomson, Judith Jarvis (1981) [1977] 'Some Ruminations on Rights', in Paul, Jeffrey (ed.) *Reading Nozick: Essays on Anarchy, State, and Utopia*, Oxford: Basil Blackwell.

Thornton, Peter (1989) *Decade of Decline, Civil Liberties in the Thatcher Years*, London: National Council for Civil Liberties.

Titmuss, Richard (1950) *Problems of Social Policy*, London: HMSO and Longmans Green.

Townsend, Sue (1989) *Mr Bevan's Dream*, London: Chatto & Windus.

Willey, Basil (1934) *The Seventeenth Century Background*, London: Penguin.

Williams, Bernard (1969) 'The Idea of Equality', in Laslett, Peter, Runciman, W.G. and Skinner, Q. (eds) *Philosophy, Politics and Society, Second Series*, Oxford: Basil Blackwell.

Williams, Bernard (1972) *Morality, An Introduction to Ethics*, Cambridge: Cambridge University Press.

Wittgenstein, Ludwig (1953) *Philosophical Investigations*, Oxford: Basil Blackwell.

Wittgenstein, Ludwig (1965) 'A Lecture on Ethics', *The Philosophical Review*, LXXIV: 3–12.

Wolff, Jonathan (1991) *Robert Nozick: Property, Justice, and the Minimal State*, Cambridge: Polity Press.

Wolff, Robert Paul (1981) [1977] 'Robert Nozick's Derivation of the Minimal State', in Paul, Jeffrey (ed.) *Reading Nozick: Essays on Anarchy, State, and Utopia*, Oxford: Basil Blackwell.

Woodhouse, A.S.P. (ed.) (1938) *Puritanism and Liberty*, London: Dent.

Index